New Creation Book for Muslims

New Creation Book for Muslims

MANDATE PRESS
Pasadena, California

© 1989 by Phil Goble and Salim Munayer
All rights Reserved

No part of this publication may be reproduced, stored in a retrieval system, or transmitted in any form or by any means—electronic, mechanical, photocopy, recording, or any other—except for brief quotations embodied in critical articles or printed reviews, without the prior permission of the publisher.

Published by
MANDATE PRESS
a subsidiary of William Carey Library
P.O. Box 40129
Pasadena, CA. 91114

All artwork and cover design by Elhanan ben Avraham

ISBN 0-87808-221-2
LC #89-061389

Printed in the United States of America

*We dedicate this book
to the Glory of Allah
who by His Merciful Compassion
to His creation
has revealed His Living Word to us
so that we might walk in the straight path*

Contents

    Dedication
1. Soiltesting   3
2. The Straight Path of the New Creation   15
3. The Prayer Life of a New Creation Muslim   69
4. The New Creation Confession   97
5. The New Creation Pilgrimage   129
6. How to Start a House Masjid for New Creation Muslims   171

Glossary   175

New Creation Book for Muslims 1
Soil Testing

1

Soiltesting

How welcome is the truth in your house?
Are you like our father *Ibrahim* (Abraham)?
When three men came to his dwelling,
Ibrahim could see who they really were
—angels in disguise.
So even though his wife laughed like a *kafir* (dis-believer),
our father Ibrahim
opened his heart
to their message[1].
Ibrahim not only recognized the truth
but he also fearlessly welcomed it.

THE FARMER AND THE FOUR KINDS OF SOIL

Different people react in different ways to the truth,
just as, when a farmer plants his seed,
various kinds of soil react variously.

---

[1] This account is found in the first book of the Torah *(Taurat)*, chapter 18. The material in the text above is intended to be read by Muslims; however, the footnotes are also directed toward those who may need additional information, because they are inexperienced in identifying with people of Muslim background.

The Parable *(Mathal)* Given

Imagine a farmer going out to plant seed.
As the farmer planted the seed,
some fell on the edge of the path,
and the birds came and ate those seeds up.
    Others fell on rocky soil
    where they sprang up quickly;
    but as soon as the sun came up,
    those that were rootless and shallow plantings
    soon withered away.
    Other seeds fell among thorns
    which grew up and choked them.
        Finally, there were seeds that fell on rich soil
        and these seeds multiplied themselves
        in the fruit they produced—
        some a hundred times over,
        some sixty times over,
        some thirty.

The Parable *(Mathal)* Explained

The truth comes like seed from a farmer's hand.
The ears that hear the truth
are like different kinds of soil
receiving the farmer's seed.
Ears without understanding hear the truth
but *Shaitan* (Satan) comes
like the birds along the path
and carries the truth away
as soon as it is planted in the hearer's heart.
Ears with fickle attention hear the truth
and welcome it at first with joy
but such a hearer has no unwavering root in himself
and he does not last;
when a crisis or a persecution comes
on account of the truth,
such a hearer falls away at once.
Ears with divided desires hear the word,
but the worries of this world,
    and the lure of riches,

Soiltesting

and the pleasures of life,
are like thorns that choke the truth
which produces in such a hearer absolutely nothing.
However, ears with understanding hear the word
like rich soil receiving seed.
Such a hearer yields a great harvest,
since a hundred or sixty or thirty times
as many hearers may receive the truth through him.
He who has ears to hear the truth
of the following *mathal* (parable), let him hear!

THE *IBN DALL* (SON OF ERROR)

There was once a *hanif* (one who desires true religion)
who had two sons.
The younger said to his father,
"Father, according to the *wasiya* (will),
let me have the *fara'id* (fixed share)
of the *mirath* (inheritance)
that is coming to me."
And the father divided his means and his property
between the younger and the elder son.
Now the elder son was a devout believer who prayed
regularly five times a day
and had made the *Hajj* (Pilgrimage) as many times.
No one was respected more among the townspeople
for his religious devotion than this elder son.
He was a man who performed his prayers
in the mosque with absolute perfection
and could read the Qur'an so well
that he would hold the audience spellbound.

THE YOUNGER SON GOES ASTRAY

It wasn't long, however, until the younger son
got everything he owned together,
and left for a far country.
There he squandered his money
in a dissolute life of *fisq* (sinfulness)
and moral depravity.
And when he had spent his entire inheritance,

and had not one thing left to remind him of his wonderful father,
there arose a terrible famine in that land;
and the younger son began to feel his loss.
So he hired himself out to a *harbi* [1]
who put him on his farm to feed the pigs.
The younger son would willingly have filled his belly
with the husks the pigs were eating
but he was treated worse than the swine,
for no one offered him even pigs' food to eat.

THE YOUNGER SON FORSAKES ALL PRIDE AND SELF-RIGHTEOUSNESS

He finally came to himself
and started thinking like an *'aqli* (rational) being,
like a true son having the disposition of his father.
He said, "How many hired servants of my father's household
abound in food and I perish with hunger!
I will arise and stop straying from *fasaqa* (the right course) and
go to my father,
and I will say to him,
"Father, I have sinned against heaven
and in the presence of you.
And I no longer think I am worthy to be called your son:
make me not like my elder brother who thinks himself worthy
but make me like one of your hired servants."
Then he arose and came to his father.

THE FATHER WHOSE LOVE MAKES THE UNRIGHTEOUS TO BE RIGHTEOUS

Now it was the tenth day
of the month of *Hajj* (Pilgrimage),
but the elder son, having a self-satisfied heart,
had some time before decided to forego the trip.
But when the younger son was yet a long way off,
his father saw him.
And greatly moved with love and compassion,
his father ran to the younger son

---

[1] A *harbi* is a non-Muslim living in territory ruled by non-Muslims.

and clasped him in his arms
and kissed him with tenderness.
And the younger son said to him,
"Father, I have sinned against heaven
and in your sight,
and I am no longer worthy to be called your son."
But the father said to his hired servants,
"Bring forth the best robe
   and put it on him;
   and put a ring on his hand
   and shoes on his feet;
   and bring the calf we have been fattening and kill it;
we are going to have
a *Qurban* (Sacrifice) as on *'Id al-Adha*[1]
such as has not been since the time Ibrahim
celebrated the redemption of *his* son.
Because this son of mine was dead
and has come back to life;
he was lost
and now he has been found."
And the great feast began.

The Elder Son Refuses to Forsake a Self-Righteous and Proud Religious Spirit

Now the elder brother
had just returned from the mosque,
and, on his way back, as he drew near the house,
he could hear the sounds of the *wisal* (communion)
of the father and his younger son.
Calling one of the hired servants,
the elder brother asked what all this was about.
And the hired servant said to the elder son,
"Your brother has returned safe and *salim* (sound)
and your father has personally sent word
for the *Qurban* (sacrifice) and the festivities to begin."

---

[1] A sacrifice without blemish is traditionally required for every free Muslim at the climax of the pilgrimage that is to be taken at least once in a lifetime, and the sacrifice is made and shared in a communion meal at the time of the major festival even by those who do not make the pilgrimage.

Now the elder brother was furious and refused to go in.
He would have nothing to do
with this sort of *din* (religious practice).
Would Allah act like his father?[1]
Would Allah bestow a *matwaba* (reward) on a son
with an innate *qariha* (disposition)
that was *asin* (rebellious)?
And not only that, one who had no *tawab* (merit)
because he had done absolutely no good deeds
or *ihsan* (right conduct)
—would Allah act like this sort of father?
The elder brother resolved to never be like such a one
and he sat down and brooded in the outer darkness.

FAILING TO RECOGNIZE THE WORD OF THE FATHER

Presently the elder brother
thought he saw another servant approaching.
But it was really his father
coming to give him a personal word[2]
in order that the elder son could start thinking
like a *'aqli* (rational) being
and enter into the spirit of the whole *jam'a'a* (house).
So his father pleaded with him.
Finally the elder son answered the man:
"Look, all these years I have submitted *islam* [3]
to you as an *abd* (slave)
and I can boast without shame that
I have religiously obeyed all of the *shari'a* (laws)
of this whole *jam'a'a* (house).
Yet I return from the mosque

---

[1] Why does the text use *God* sometimes and *Allah* other times? Because the elder brother is presented as a Muslim in the story, and as a Muslim he would naturally favor the Arabic word for *God*.

[2] *Kalim* is the Quranic term for "word." Since Isa is called Allah's Word in the Qur'an 4:171 and since he is also the personal Word who took the form of a servant, the word choice is important here in English. Some of these parenthetical words are cues to the Arabic translator and some are added for nuance.

[3] See note 2 above.

and I hear the sounds of the *wisal* (communion)
between you and this *mufarrit* (prodigal)!
Am I now to humble myself
and enter a house with this sort of *zamala* (fellowship)?"

A COSTLY DEATH AND THE INHERITANCE OF THE FATHER'S PERSONAL WORD TO HIS HEIRS

Then the father looked at him with anguished love
and said,
"You know the costly death a *murith* (testator)
must somehow undergo in order that his heirs
may receive all that he has.
And yet you seem to love me
more like a self-justifying slave
than a trusting and humble son."
The father put his arm around the man and said,
"Are you so far away from knowing me
that you cannot rejoice that the one
who strayed from the *fasaqa* (right course)
has found *tajaddud* (renewal)
and has been *rashid* (rightly guided)
to the *marashid* (salvation) of Allah?
For *like you*
your brother had a *sajiya* (natural disposition)
that was dead but now he has been *jadda* (restored)
to the abundant life of *wisal* (communion)
as an heir of his father's house."[1]

ARE YOU WILLING TO RECEIVE THE NEW CREATION HEART,
THE HEART OF A LITTLE CHILD,
THE HEART THAT RECOGNIZES THE TRUTH?

Have you not read what it says of Isa al-Masih
that he would "heal those born blind

---

[1] Dr. Kenneth Bailey has written *The Cross and the Prodigal*, published by Concordia, dramatizing how a Muslim might see the Cross of Christ in Luke 15.

and the lepers...and raise the dead?"[1]
Why did he do this for people?
Because it says in the *Zabur* (Psalms)
that Allah "would send his Word and heal them
and deliver them from the Pit of *jahannam*"[2] (hell fire)
Have you not read,
"The Messiah, Isa, Jesus son of Mary,
was the *Rasul* (Messenger) of Allah, and his Word"[3] ?
Allah has always loved his Word
as a father loves his only son.
And his Word has always been
the *sirr* (secret) of the mind of Allah,
as a son is the likeness of his father.
What blasphemer would breathe the name of Mary here?
She was nothing but a loaner of flesh,
for Allah has no wife and no mother and no partner
nor did He need any human being at all
to be what He has always been,
the one and only God.

ONLY A CHILD-LIKE HEART RECOGNIZES THE TRUTH

Now the story goes that Isa who is Allah's Word
had been healing many people in *Muqaddasa* (the Holy Land).
And when he sat down,
each *talib* (seeker) also brought unto Isa
his *walad* (little child)
in order for him to pronounce the *baraka* (blessing).
And so, with tender love, Isa,
who reverberates the love of the heart of Allah,
picked each one up

---

[1] Family of 'Imran. 3:49. All references in English are from A. Yusuf Ali: *The Holy Qur'an*, first published 1934. Those who, for whatever reason, object to the frequent quotations from the Qur'an in this book should remember that Paul quotes "one of their prophets" verbatim in order to win the citizens of Crete when what "one of their prophets" said lines up with the Word. See Titus 1:12-13. This book follows the rather unorthodox route of Pauline methodology.
[2] Psalm 107:20
[3] Women.4:171

Soiltesting 11

and placed the *walad* (little child)
one at a time on his lap.
Just then his *hawari* (disciples)
impatiently interrupted him and told the parents
that they would have to leave.
But Isa loved little children who, as everyone knows,
humbly and whole-heartedly receive what is given to them.
Little children accept everything as a gift
with awestruck gratitude as if from the hand of Allah,
and not with any tendency
to think they deserve God's favor on the basis of merit,
since in their own small eyes
they wisely know themselves too little
to have done any good deeds.
Isa said,
"Allow the little children to come unto me
and forbid them not.
For it is to people with hearts like these
that the *Malakut* (Kingdom) of God belongs.
In very truth I say to you,
whosoever shall not welcome
the *Malakut* (Kingdom) of Allah
like a *walad* little child ,
will never enter it."[1]

THE TRUTH HAS *NOT* BEEN LOST IN TRANSCRIPTION SINCE EVEN LITTLE CHILDREN CAN RECOGNIZE THE FATHER'S PERSONAL WORD OF TRUTH

Isa had difficulty with his people,
because many suppressed the correct interpretation
of the Scriptures that spoke of his coming.
However, those who did attempt to "conceal
Allah's revelations in the Book"[2] did not succeed
as a Muslim child proved in 1947
when he discovered the Dead Sea Scrolls.
Extremely ancient parts of every book (but one)
of the Hebrew Bible were found there in manuscript form,

---

[1] Luke 18:15-17
[2] Cow 2:174

greatly discrediting the skeptical scholars who had attacked its infallible accuracy and reliability.[1]

ARE YOU WILLING TO READ THE ANCIENT PROPHETS WITH THE HUMBLE HEART OF A LITTLE CHILD?[2]

---

[1] These two thousand year old but newly discovered documents show that the scribal transcription has been trustworthy enough to insure that the original message has not been lost, for "none can change Allah's Words" (Cave 18:27). The Arab Bedouin who found (near the Dead Sea at Qumran) the scroll of Isaiah, the most important prophet of both the Hebrew and the Christian Bible, provided the world with scientific proof that the Bible has not been corrupted and lost. For this two-thousand year old perfectly preserved scroll matches our own version, proving that the original has *not* been lost in scribal transcription.

[2] Anyone has permission to duplicate the material in this section for free distribution.

2

The Straight Path of the New Creation

Allah knows where you live
and so do *Shaitan* and the evil *jinn* (demons).
This was proven to a man of God
in modern times.

This is a true story.

A PRAYER IS MIRACULOUSLY ANSWERED

The man of God was calling out to Allah one morning
to bring more people to the *jami'* (congregation).
He was on his face before Allah
and he was supplicating *du'a* very loudly
alone in a tiny apartment.
This was the only *masjid* (place of prayer)
the people had for their meetings
because the godless leaders,
more sensitive to politics than to Allah,
had thrown the congregation
out of a public meeting hall.

But praise be to Allah who hears and answers
when we call on Him!
There is none like the Lord our God,
praise be unto Him.
He says somewhere,
"Before they call I will answer;

and while they are yet speaking I will hear."
In fact, the request of the man of God
had been answered *weeks before* he made his petition.

HOW GOD HAD BEEN PREPARING TO ANSWER PRAYER

Here is the true story:
A young man and his wife
had been travelling for several days
looking for the man of God.
Allah had led them on a spiritual pilgrimage,
for Allah foreknew both the prayer and its answer,
which He was now effecting.

We will call these two *muridun* (aspirants)
Isha and Ahmad.
They had long heard of the spiritual *'ilm* (knowledge)
of the man of God,
though they had never met him personally.
And so they went out like *Ibrahim* (Abraham),
"who by faith obeyed
when he was called to go out to a place
which he was to receive as an inheritance;
and he went out,
not knowing where he was to go."

Like Ibrahim, the man and wife wanted to seek
the straight path,
the path of the just,
and they sought to do this
under the *huda* (guidance) of the man of God.

The man and woman wanted to submit their lives to Allah
and find the path of life in His Word,
as it says,
"Make me to go in the path of thy commandments,
for therein do I delight."

However, Isha and Ahmad did not know in which village
the man of God lived,
nor the street location of his dwelling.

But praise be to Allah
for it says,
"Thy word is a lamp unto my feet
and a light unto my path."

THE MIRACLE OCCURS

On the very night before the miracle happened,
Ahmad and Isha happened to take a room in a hotel
a very short distance from the place
where the man of God dwelt.

On the very morning
when the man of God
was petitioning Allah so earnestly to send more people,
Isha had taken her baby for a walk
and she was going down the street.

She was walking along,
and when she came to the building
where the man of God was on his face
crying out to God
(even though there was no sign on the building
nor any way in the world to know
the man of God was inside)
Isha stopped and asked a lady passer-by
if she knew of any *jami'* *(gath*ering)
for *du'a* (free-prayer) in the area.

The lady passer-by happened to be a *murid* (novice believer)
who belonged to the persecuted flock of Allah
that met in the dwelling of the man of God.

Not only that,
the women happened,
in the providence of Allah,
to pass each other
right in front of this very house *masjid* (place of prayer)!

"The Lord orders the steps of a righteous person"
is the saying.
Many err with their doctrine

knowing neither the Scriptures nor the power of God,
nor the love of God, which passes all understanding.
What Allah foreknows He forewills
"to work together for good for those
who love Allah, who are called according to his purpose,"
who are blessed, because they "are not offended at His Word."

At this exact moment, then,
just as the man of God finished his petition
with the words, "Send us more people, Lord"
—there was a knock on the door!

The man of God had no idea who Isha was.
"Do you know where my husband and I
could find a congregation?" Isha asked.

"Yes," the man of God said, flabbergasted.
"Praise to Him," Isha said,
"because we've been seeking
to find a certain man of God,"
and then she gave his name.
"Do you know where I could find him?"
"I'm he," the man of God said.
"Oh..." Isha was shocked.

So the man of God saw his prayer
answered so suddenly and miraculously.

God had led the woman to the man of God.
Al-Hadi (The Guide) knew where he lived!
For *Al-Hadi* is *Al-'Alim* (The All-Knowing).

Right after that the congregation started to grow again,
despite the opposition of the godless.
And both Isha and her husband Ahmad
submitted to the death *ghusl*
of New Creation Islam in the ocean,
calling on Allah to cleanse their inner being
with "the *wudu* (washing) of *tajaddud* (regeneration)
and the renewing of the Eternal Spirit of Allah."
That was nearly ten years ago.
Then the man of God moved to another place.

The Straight Path of the New Creation

YEARS LATER ANOTHER MIRACLE HAPPENS

Would it take a miracle
to show you the difference
between a true Islamic teacher
and a pseudo-Islamic teacher?

Very recently Ahmad called the man of God
long distance on the telephone to tell him
that Isha wanted a divorce.
They had been having marriage problems
and she had turned to a man for help,
a fraud who claimed to be a good *murshid* (spiritual guide)
but who was in reality
a pseudo-Islamic *shaman*
trafficking in the realm of spells
and charms and sorcery,
witchcraft, talismans and familiar spirits,
divining, saint worship, and demons,
fortune-telling, incantations and the evil eye.

It says somewhere,
"Acquaint now thyself with Him (Allah)
and be at peace;
thereby good shall come unto Thee."

But some people want to get more acquainted
with *jinn* or demons rather than the Word of Allah,
as it says,
"My people perish for lack of knowledge of Thy word,
for they have rejected the knowledge of thy Word."

The *haram* (forbidden) demon procurer
whom Isha consulted
promised her peace
and even dramatic out-of-the-body psychic experiences;
he claimed to offer her direct access
to "Spiritual Masters" who make their appearance
as "light-being entities."

Such counterfeit guides, as this man, are like

the devils with whom they commune.
They are unclean religious peddlers
disguised as servants of Allah.
There is nothing unexpected about such frauds
if, as it says,
"*Shaitan* himself goes disguised as an angel of light
seeking whom he may devour."

THE MAN OF GOD DECIDES TO TEACH ISHA AND AHMAD
ABOUT MARRIAGE IN TERMS OF THE KINGDOM

"Blessed be He in whose hands is the Kingdom...."[1]
And blessed indeed are the hands of Him
into whom all the power of the Kingdom
is given: the Word of Allah.
Yet the Kingdom of Allah
is not in word,
but in power
—not the words of dying men,
nor the might of fleeting worldly power.
Did not the living Word of Allah himself declare,
"My Kingdom is not of this world;
if my Kingdom were of this world,
then would my servants fight *jihad* ".[2]
The Kingdom of Allah is in the power of His Word.
And what does His Word say?
The whole story swept through the mind of the man of God...

ALLAH HAS ACTED MIGHTILY TO BRING US TO HIS KINGDOM

From the good beginning
mankind has swerved
from the straight path
of Allah and his Word.

From the first commandment

---

[1] Kingdom 67:11. All Quranic references in English are from A. Yusuf Ali: *The Holy Qur'an*, first published in 1934.
[2] *Jihad* means to strive in the way of God. What is often called "holy war" is only one meaning of the term.

given beneath the tree
of the knowledge of good and evil
mankind has acted shadily
toward Allah and his Glory.

And what is Allah's Glory
if not the Word of his Power?
And what is his glorious Power
if not the Word of his Presence?
One of your prophets has said rightly:
"The Messiah, Isa, Jesus son of Mary,
was the Messenger of Allah, and his Word
that he bestowed on Mary."[1]
But His Word that He bestowed on Mary
went forth from His mouth
at the creation of the world.
    For in the beginning
    was the Word
    and the Word was with God
    and the Word
    was God.[2]
The Power and the Presence was
Allah's Only Eternal Word;
and everything was made
by the Word,
and without the Word
was nothing made.
Then the Word
came on the scene
as a human being
who is true Man
on the straight path
to the tree of life.
And his disciples beheld his glory,
glory as of the only
personal and eternal Word of Allah,
full of grace and truth.

---

[1] Women 4:171
[2] John 1:1

What blasphemer would breathe the name of Mary here
as one of the "gods in derogation of God"?[1]
Are you so slow in understanding
that you think we believe Allah got married?
What blasphemy!
Who could believe that Allah would take a wife?
Do you think we mean that the Word of Allah
is His Son in that literal sense?
Not at all!
Mary was nothing but a loaner of flesh![2]
For Allah has neither wife nor mother nor partner
nor did He ever need a human being at all
to be what He has always been—one!

Allah always existed with His Everlasting Word
and His Everlasting Spirit as *tawhid* (one).
What blasphemer would assert otherwise?
Would you be so foolish as to say
that Allah once existed without His Eternal and Living Word
and without His Everlasting Spirit?
Would you have Allah at one time mute
and unable to utter a living Word?
Would you have Him at one time Spiritless,
without His Eternal Spirit?

---

[1] Qur'an 5:116 is against the worship of Mary, which Epiphanius tells us the Collyridians practiced in Arabia. Sura 5:77/73 and similar references are against tritheism—three gods—a doctrine true believers have always rejected. God is one, but He has always had personal distinctions within Himself that included His Word and His Eternal Holy Spirit. See Sura 4:171 for a reference to "His Word" Isa or Jesus and see 5:110 for a reference to His Holy Spirit.

[2] This teaching cannot be overemphasized. The terms "Father" and "Son" are human analogies or metaphors to give some understanding of God as He relates personally to His Word and as His Word relates personally to Him. These terms do not indicate polytheism as the daughters of God did in Sura 53:19-21. In Sura 9:30 the title "Son of God" is objected to because it is seen as reflecting the earlier polytheism too. Nor should the title imply physical paternity, a concept opposed by Sura 6:101. The word "Father" is metaphorical as in the Arabic name *Abu 'l-Barakat,* the Father of Blessings. Likewise the word "Son" is metaphorical in the Quranic designation Ibn al-Sabil, son of the road, hence traveler. Sura 2:215

The Straight Path of the New Creation

Such blasphemers would do to the imaginary God they worship
what they would not dream of doing to themselves
—namely, cut out all living utterance and life
to be left with a mere speechless, lifeless being.
If only these dreamers would wake up from such nonsense
and shut their mouths to save their souls!
Instead they pride themselves
that their speechless, Spiritless deity has no 'partners'!

When Allah speaks His mind He speaks His Word,
for His Word is the revealed mind of Allah.
And we can have His mind in all things
if we die to our own way of thinking
and come alive to His living Word.

The man of God reflected on Isha and Ahmad
and how they must learn
to think the thoughts of the mind
revealed to us in the sacred pages of the Word.
For it was in His image that we were created
and it is from His glory that we have fallen,
having become futile in our thinking
and darkened in our senseless minds.

But if we are now more like brute beasts
(because of the ignorance that is in us
and the blindness of our hearts),
it is not because He made us so.
For Allah gave us not an animal mind
but a mind like His,
a rational and a creative mind
capable of communion with Him in Holiness.

OUR RELIGION CLOAKS OUR DARK GUILT

However, our sinful nature has separated us
from our Holy God
and, obeying the voice of the Evil One,
we ourselves have become evil,
though we love to hide our guilt
under the cloak of religion.
But Allah is not mocked.

All things are naked and opened
unto the eyes of Him
with whom we have to do.
He who made the eye,
can He not see?
And even the scoffers know
that we are of our father the devil
if the lusts of our father we do.

Only the Word of Allah
can speak into our hearts
a new creation nature!
As long as we place our trust
in anything apart from the living Word,
that "anything" becomes our real god
and we become its slaves.
No matter how religiously
we observe religious rules and laws,
that idol "anything" has usurped
the living Word's place in our hearts
and will lead us to corruption.

Now religious do's and don'ts
were the rudimentary guardians
of our spiritual childhood, it is true.
But the time has come
for us to outgrow the tutelage
of mere religious formalism
and to receive the spiritual adoption
of mature heirs.
When the living Word
takes up residence within us,
we receive a filial spirit of obedience;
we become the spiritual people of Ibrahim,
and God becomes our Father.
For God sent his living Word
into our hearts to restore us
in his likeness and for his fellowship,
that we might walk naturally with Him as our Father,
and not hobble like aliens under the cold prod of laws.

The Man of God Thinks About How to Save Isha's Marriage

The man of God thought about Isha
and how she must learn to understand God's forgiveness.
It is not that we love God and serve him with such grace
that we can be assured of forgiveness
based on what we have done for God.
No, it is that God loves us and has served us with such grace
that the Judge of sin has taken the whole weight
of our guilt and condemnation upon Himself.
The Word of Allah's eternal Judgment became also
the Word of His eternal Mercy!

But how?
In the person of His Word, Isa al-Masih.
Thus it is that we can be assured of forgiveness,
based on what God has done for us,
in giving us a new mind with His Word,
and a tender conscience with His Eternal Spirit.

Allah has always reflected upon Himself with His wisdom,
and His wisdom is His Word.[1]

Isa al-Masih Himself *is* that Word!
He is the everlasting Word
whose words will stand forever.[2]
The *Kitab* (Book) of Isa is Genesis to Revelation,
infallibly accurate in its teaching about him,
and Isa is the hidden source and subject of each *sura* (chapter)
for those who can read with the eyes of the Eternal Spirit.

As a word reveals the hidden mind of a father,
so Allah intended this mind to be in us

---

[1] No true prophet before Isa ever claimed to know God, just to have heard from Him or caught a glimpse of Him. In Matthew 11:27 Isa claims what only the personal Word of God can claim: fullness of knowledge of God. This is significant to readers of the Qur'an, since nowhere in the Qur'an does it say that the Injil has a faulty text.

[2] Matthew 24:35

that was also in his Word.[1]

But the mirror of our reflection of His holiness
has been shattered,
and the whole human race has distorted itself
in mocking pride and rebellion
against the humble and obedient Word.

As a sin-fallen race
we still possess a vestige of the mirror of conscience.
Like a looking-glass before the mind,
the conscience tells the human race
how good we might have been
had Man not warped himself
in the refractive beams of Man's proud self-love.
Therefore, we are without excuse when we reject
any measure of truth we receive.

Our sin-prone race is like someone
who once was commanded to peer
at his Ideal in a full-length mirror
and then disobediently walked away
and forgot what he looked like.
Isa the Word of Allah is that Ideal.
And the fatherly heart of Allah
out of whom the Word spoke in the beginning
has been stirred to speak again
to the lost family of Adam:
"I reared sons, I brought them up,
but they have rebelled against me."

For the Word became
the One who was to come,
the heavenly Son of Man,
the *Bar Nasha* (Aramaic for Son of Man).[2]

---

[1] Philippians 2:5

[2] The "Son of Man" is the name the prophet Daniel gave to the Messiah-figure Allah showed him in a vision. This One Daniel saw was given the divine authority to judge the whole world and yet the figure in the vision looked like a human being. Isa used the term "Son of Man" as a description

The Straight Path of the New Creation

The prophet Daniel saw him
in the clouds of glory and wrote:
"After this I saw in the night visions
and, behold, one like the Son of Man
came with the clouds of heaven...
and he was given...a kingdom...
that all people, nations, and languages
should serve him."[1]
The Word that was in the beginning with God,
the Word that was God,
this same Word was made flesh
and dwelt among us,
telling his disciples,
"Verily, verily, I say unto you,
Hereafter you shall see heaven open
and the angels of God
ascending and descending upon the Son of Man."[2]
For the Word of Allah had come
to speak into a new existence our dying humanity.
And just as Man had gone down to death
in the Garden of Eden
as one conquered by Satan and sin,
so now Man may ascend again to life
from the empty Garden tomb
through One who overcame for us,
through One who conquered as our *imam* (leader),
our representative,
our exemplar,
—a human being who is that
and yet more than human,
sharing in the wholly other quality of God,
the eternal personal Word of Allah,
God the Word from God the Lord,

---

of himself. It was his favorite messianic title. The 1947 discovery of the two thousand year old Dead Sea Scrolls contains several passages from Daniel. These passages are scientific proof that Daniel's prophecy was not lost in erroneous scribal transcription and that our copies of this prophecy are reliable.

[1] Daniel 7:13-14
[2] John 1:51

Light from Light,
Very God from Very God.

Since this is true
—that the Word who is
　and was
　and is to come,
the Word who is
　the express thought of God,
　the perfect image of God,
　the creative voice of God
—since this very Word
descended so that He might dwell
in our hearts by faith
and make us like Him,
restoring us in the image of His Father
that we might call on His Father as sons,
that we might ascend with Him,
passing beyond the angels
(Do you not know that we shall judge angels?)
—since this is true,
should it not teach us that,
denying ungodliness and worldly lusts,
we should live sober,
righteous, and godly lives
in this present world?
Since the Word Himself revealed to us
perfect surrender to Allah and
total submission to His will,
only through Him and His *iman* (faith),
once for all delivered to the holy ones,
do we know what is possible to man
in the path of obedience to the one true God.

Thus the man of God reflected on the straight path
and on Isha and Ahmad
and on their battle against *Shaitan*.

ALLAH BOUND UP THE EVIL ONE

The man of God knew that the Kingdom of God

is an *ummah*, (community)[1]
a house to be entered
by the narrow gate and the narrow door.
But a "strong man" has usurped power in God's House.
Iblis (an evil prince) has held men captive
in the house of Allah,
and *Iblis* must have his goods plundered
before men can be set free from his sway.
The power of *Iblis* is death,
for all men who are tempted and sin
die as punishment.
Sin pays its fearful wage—death.
Death is the fearful wage of all those
whom *Shaitan* has led to work for him in sin.
Therefore, only by plundering the goods of the strong man,
—that is, by taking away his power
to enslave men in the fear of death
and his power to tempt men to destruction,
according to the law of sin and death
—only by plundering these goods
could the Word of Allah defeat *Iblis*.
Thus it says of the Word of Allah, Isa,
that "by his death he could take away all the power of the devil,
who had power over death."

The Good News that the man of God proclaimed
is this very power,
the power of spiritual life over spiritual death,
the power that delivers us from every evil
and will soon rescue us from the presence of wickedness
when all things shall be subdued unto the Word of Allah
and the Word Himself also shall be subject unto Him
that put all things under His Word,
that Allah may be All in All exalted.[2]
But when the Word of Allah, Isa, returns,
shall He find faith on the earth?

---

[1] The messianic *ummah* is the one people of Allah who are the new creation sons of Ishmael and Abraham in one family, the redeemed spiritual community of God and hence the citizens of the Kingdom of God.

[2] See I Corinthians 15:27-28.

For many of the Jewish people did not believe his report;
and since the Word of Allah did not reign in their hearts
he was despised and rejected as their king,
and they esteemed not his kingdom.
"But when they said (in boast)
'We killed Isa al-Masih,
the son of Mary,
the Messenger of God,'
they killed him not,
nor crucified him,
but so it was made
to *appear* to them..."[1]
It only *appeared*
that *men and not God* determined His death.
For "it pleased *the Lord* to crush Him!"
Allah it was "who caused him to suffer,"
as the prophet foretold.[2]
Isa al-Masih Himself confessed and denied not,
"No *man* taketh my life from me,
but I lay it down of my own free will,
and as it is in my power to lay my life down,
so it is in my power to take it up again." (John 10:18)
Did you not know that the Word of Allah willingly died?
For this end was He born
and for this cause did He die
and for this alone did Allah send Him into the world:
Allah so loved the world
that He gave His only living Word
as a sin-covering sacrifice,
"a momentous sacrifice,"
as it reads in the saying,
"Behold! Allah said:
'O Jesus! I will take thee
and I (raise) thee to Myself...' "[3] .
Have you not read that the Jewish people promised Allah

---

[1] Women 4:157

[2] Isaiah 53:10. The entire book of Isaiah has been incorruptibly preserved in the Dead Sea Scrolls, leaving no doubt that this text is not a forgery but the very Word of Allah!

[3] Family of 'Imran 3:55

"not to believe in a Messenger
unless He showed us a sacrifice" [1]?
And have you not read that Allah
who is rich in mercy,
for His great love wherewith He loved us
even when we were dead in sins
(like sheep led to the slaughter,
like Ibrahim's son led to the slaughter),
that Allah so loved the world
that he ransomed Ibrahim's doomed progeny
—"and We ransomed him
with a momentous sacrifice"?[2]

Are you ignorant of the prophecy of Isaiah
(sealed incorruptibly in the Dead Sea Scrolls
and fulfilled 700 years later
in the death of Isa al-Masih):
"Yet it was the Lord's will to crush him
and cause him to suffer,
and though the Lord makes his life
a sacrifice offering for sin,
he (the Masih) will see his (spiritual) progeny,

---

[1] Family of 'Imran 3:183

[2] Ranks 37:107 Some may say that this verse is being quoted out of context, since it originally referred to Ibrahim, his son, and the ram. However, Isa himself said that "these same Scriptures—meaning the Torah accounts including this story about Abraham—refer to me."(John 5:39) Everything written about him (Isa) in the Law of Moses had to be fulfilled, according to Isa's own words in Luke 24:44. The interpretation of the Messiah himself was that Noah, Joseph, and Ibrahim's son, etc., are all properly interpreted to be prophetic foreshadowings of Isa. Therefore, if the Qur'an refers to stories or characters in the Law of Moses, then since the original context in the Taurat refers prophetically to Isa, it is arbitrary and wrong to exclude this meaning from the Qur'an. A true prophet does not go beyond what is written (I Corinthians 4:6). If Isa is present in the original Biblical context, Isa cannot be erased in any subsequent reference to that context, whether in the Qur'an or elsewhere. Notice that in this Qur'anic reference we are talking about a substitutionary sacrifice. Qur'anic commentators who disagree can be dismissed because they are not prophets and their comments do not carry prophetic authority. This is true also of their Qur'anic interpretation that says Isa did not die.

he shall prolong his days,
and the will of the Lord
will prosper in his hand.
After the suffering of his soul,
he (the Masih) will see the light of (resurrection) life
and be satisfied;
by his knowledge my righteous servant[1]
will make many just,
taking their faults on himself."[2]

Are we, then, not that doomed progeny of Ibrahim?
"No indeed.
Allah raised him (Jesus) up unto Himself..."[3]
And Allah has brought us
spiritually alive together with Isa
(by grace we are saved)
and has raised us up together
as the spiritual progeny of Ibrahim
and made us sit together
in the triumph of his eternal *ummah* (community).
Therefore, when the iniquity
of this present world is complete,
this same living Word
who was taken up to heaven
shall also come again
in like manner as He went.
And then it shall be as it says,
"The Day the heaven is split asunder with the clouds,
and the angels are sent down in ranks,
that day, the kingdom, the true kingdom, shall belong
to the All-merciful, and it shall be a day harsh
for the unbelievers"...[4]
"And (Isa) shall be
a Sign (for the coming of) the Hour (of Judgment):

---

[1] "Isa said:'I am indeed a servant of Allah...' "Mary 19:30
[2] Isaiah 53:10-11
[3] Women. 4:158
[4] Criterion 25:25-26

The Straight Path of the New Creation

Therefore have no doubt about the (Hour)"...[1]
"And thy Lord shall come with angels,
rank on rank." (Daybreak 89:22)

On that day the Word of Allah will fight.
That will be the day of his *jihad,* his holy war.
And the Word of Allah will slay *al-Masih al-Dajjal,*
the False Messiah, and his lying prophet,
together with all who have lying visions
and all who consult them
or have come bringing a different doctrine
that is not the teaching of Isa al-Masih.

On that day it shall be as was seen
by *Yahya,* (John) one of Isa's *hawari rusul* (apostles):
"And I saw heaven opened,
and behold a white horse;
and He that sat upon it was called
Faithful and True,
and in righteousness he doth judge and make war.
His eyes were as a flame of fire
and on his head were many crowns;
and he had a name written,
that no man knew, but he himself.
And he was clothed with a vesture dipped in blood:
and his name is called
The Word of God." (Revelation 19:11-13)
This same Word is coming again
with the armies of the angels of God.
He is coming to punish the unbelieving wicked
and to save the faithful who endure to the end.
So then the Kingdom will be the Lord's.

Therefore, if death entered humanity
by the sin of the first man,
life from the dead entered humanity
by the righteousness of the new man,
the Word of Allah,
who came as a man

---

[1] Ornaments 43:61

to bind *Shaitan* and plunder his goods
by offering a death that would free all men
   from the fear of death,
   from the power of death,
   from the realm of death,
   from the law of death.

For whoever believes in Isa the Word of Allah
will not see the death
reserved for *Shaitan*,
the second death,
in the lake of fire.

For since one man died in the place of all
all then died in that one man,
and *Shaitan* now has no dominion over those
who overcome him by the blood of the Word of Allah,
Isa al-Masih.
Such are they who overcome *Shaitan* by the good confession
of their testimony to the grace of Isa al-Masih
who saves us from the second death in the lake of fire.

It was then that the man of God saw the mystery
of how to fight *Shaitan*.
This is the mystery of the narrow door
into the House of Allah.
This is the small gate
into the Kingdom of Allah.
It is the blood of the Word,
it is the death of Isa al-Masih
and few there be who find it.

For Isa Himself said,
"Enter through the narrow gate.
For wide is the gate
and broad is the road
that leads to destruction,
and many enter through it.
But small is the gate
and narrow the road
that leads to life,
and only a few find it." (Matthew 7:13)

ALLAH SHOWS THE MAN OF GOD HOW TO FIGHT SHAITAN

After Ahmad telephoned the man of God
to tell about Isha consulting the false *murshid* (spiritual guide)
and his "Spiritual Master light beings,"
the man of God went to bed and fell into a deep sleep.

About three o'clock in the morning
a voice spoke to the man of God.
It spoke so loud the man of God woke up instantly
and was wide awake.

It was a deeply resonant, masculine,
and yet feminine-sounding voice
and it said only one short syllable,
an ugly little word
the man of God didn't recognize.
Nevertheless, it blasted in his ears
and woke him up.

The man of God opened his eyes,
and the whole room where he had been sleeping
was pulsating with a scarlet light,
as brilliant as a strobe light.
The room was normally pitch black
at three o'clock in the morning
but now everything in the room was brightly visible.
The man of God stood up
to make sure he was awake.
The awesome light of this
definite supernatural visitation continued.

Then the Lord seemed to speak
to the man of God in a very still small voice,
"This is the demon she prays to.
Cover yourself with the blood of my Word Isa."[1]

---

[1] What this idea refers to is the authority Isa al-Masih has over the demonic priniciplaities and powers because of the victory He won on the cross as the Word of God. For he provided a death for us that takes away Satan's power over us, the fear of death resulting from sin. But though sin and death

The man of God instantly saw the nature
of the spritual struggle:
the demon was attacking the man of God
because Isha was his property
and this devil was protecting his goods.

The man of God said these simple words with faith,
"I cover myself with the blood of Isa."

Immediately the pulsating light faded.

"Resist the Devil," it says somewhere;
"overcome him by the confession of your faith in Isa
and by the blood of Isa,
and he will flee from you."

The man of God lay down and closed his eyes.
Immediately he saw
with the vision given him by the Eternal Spirit of Allah
a package in the house of Isha and Ahmad.

The indwelling Spirit of Allah
impressed on the mind of the man of God
that he should call Ahmad on the telephone right then
and tell him to go back into his house,
taking dominion over it room by room,
covering the realm of his dominion
with the blood of Allah's *halifa* (agent in charge),
Isa the Word of Allah.
It was especially impressed on the man of God
that Ahmad was to cover his wife Isha
with the blood of the Word of Allah
and get that horrible package of occult materials
out of their house.
Whatever was in that package,
whether it was charms made out of pieces of writing
or hair-cuttings or nail-trimmings or the hand of Fatima

---

caught us in a Devilish cycle, righteousness and life come to us through faith in the Word of God and His death and resurrection for our salvation. See Hebrews 2:14-15; James 1:14-15; Colossians 2:15; Ephesians 6:11-12; Revelation 12:11.

The Straight Path of the New Creation

or knots or magic or material for sorcery
or any other wicked thing,
whether it was any curse or blessing
thought to ward off the evil eye,
any practice or object that grieves the Eternal Spirit of Allah
—these must all be curtailed and destroyed;
as it says,
"Thou canst not stand before thine enemies,
(until) ye take away the accursed thing from among you."[1]
Whoever puts his hand to the plow
but then keeps looking back at this Satanic wickedness
is not fit for the Kingdom of Allah.
It would be better to enter heaven with nothing
than to enter hell with all these filthy possessions.
For without holiness no man will see God.
And if you leave the door open by keeping this filth
in your possession,
any demon that is cast out will go and find seven other demons
and come back to drag you down to hell.

The man of God obeyed the Lord.
Even though it was not yet four o'clock in the morning,
the man of God called Ahmad and woke him up.
The man of God covered him
with the blood of the Word of Allah
and called out to God, interceding for him on the telephone.

When Ahmad heard what had happened to the man of God
he realized that this demon who had taken over his house,
who was destroying the peace of his family
and unsettling his children,
this demon who was oppressing his wife,
this same demon was trying to frighten the man of God away
from saving their home.
Ahmad also promised the man of God
that he would not sign the divorce papers
that very day as his wife had requested.

---

[1] Joshua 7:13

The admonition is clear:
"Pray at all times in the Spirit."

To pray in the Spirit means to pray in the power of the Spirit,
with the gifts of the Spirit potentially in evidence.
When the man of God saw the package,
it was by means of a gift of the Eternal Spirit of Allah;
namely, supernatural "knowledge" [1]
—that is, supernaturally provided knowledge
that he could not acquire by means of his natural mind.

"For we are not battling
against personalities made of flesh and blood,
but against beings without bodies
—the evil overlords of the unseen world,
those mighty demonic beings
and great evil rulers of darkness who dominate this world;
and against hordes of wicked spirits
in the spirit world."[2]

HOW TO ADMIT THE INFALLIBLE RELIABILITY OF THE WORD

We must receive a new spirit,
a spirit like the Eternal Spirit.
For God will be faithful
only with the faithful[3] and His pure light
will shine forth from the Word only for the pure.
With the wicked who fail to tremble at His Word,
God is angry every day[4]
Like many long ago who were quick
to accuse Isa al-Masih of error
but were slow to see error in themselves,
so today these vile unbelievers are quick
to do the same with His written Word.

---

[1] I Corinthians 12:8
[2] Ephesians 6:12
[3] Psalm 18:26. But see also II Tim. 2:13.
[4] Yet God is long-suffering to us, not willing that any should perish, but that all should come to repentance. See II Peter 3:9.

The natural man cannot understand the words of the Spirit;
they are beyond him,
they are foolishness to him.
How can anyone understand
what is eternal and spiritually discerned
if he lacks the Eternal Spirit?
Reading is not enough;
the words are straight but the reader is crooked.
The reader must be reborn and be set on the straight path,
not by mere human resolve but by the will of God.[1]

A WORD ABOUT JUDAS AND THOSE LIKE HIM

How can anyone read what is godly
if he himself is devilish?
Could Judas "read" Jesus?
Even though Judas sat next to the Word of Allah
eating his bread at the Last Supper,
all Judas could read were "errors."
Judas had frequently heard Jesus say
that it was necessary for the Messiah to die
as a sacrifice for the sins of the world,
but Judas "read" this solemn declaration as an error.

"The Messiah must be strong to rule us,"
Judas thought, "not weak."
"How can he be anybody important
if he's going to die instead of lead an army?
His errors will get us *all* killed, not just himself!"
Isa had enough love to die for Judas' sins
but, like the rest of unregenerate humanity,
Judas saw error in this and in everything else
except in his own black heart.

Bitter sons of the devil!
Black-hearted traitors against God
who take sides with Judas
against the infallibly accurate Word of Allah!

---

[1]John 1:13

But some fools are even more perverse!
Who is more truly a liar
than the one who would make this devil Judas
who committed suicide in shame and utter ignominy
the one who was crucified in Isa's place?[1]

Such a one will surely go the way of Judas
for agreeing with him
that God's account of things cannot be trusted.
Only a *good* man like Isa could cry out
while hanging on the *khashabah* (wood) in the agony of death,
"My God, my God, why hast thou forsaken me?"
A traitor like Judas would know the answer to that question!

Isa said of Judas, "It would have been better
if that man had never been born."
And if like Judas we think ourselves wiser
than the Word of Allah,
it would have been better
if such an error as us had never been born!
Isa was willing to die that same day for Judas
but Judas refused to pick up his cross and die,
if necessary, with Isa.
Judas saw an error in that.
What craftiness this fool had!
He saw he could save his own life
and even make some money
just by betraying Isa
to the wicked priestly rulers who were looking to kill him.
But whoever tries to save his life will lose it.[2]
Only those who lose their lives in *islam* (surrender) to Isa
will find their lives and keep them for eternity.

Judas was the first apostle to lose his life,
and he also lost his soul,
as it says,

---

[1] Note that this is only one Muslim interpretation and not all Muslims have believed this lie.
[2] Matthew 16:25

The Straight Path of the New Creation

"Let his habitation be desolate."[1]
He missed seeing the Messiah's resurrection by only a few hours!
But his fall was predicted
by the prophet *Da'ud* (David) in the *Zabur* (Psalms)
as part of the sufferings to be endured by the Messiah:
"Yes, mine own familiar friend, in whom I trusted,
which did eat of my bread,
hath lifted up his heel against me."[2]
But the Word of Allah who delivered this prophecy to *Da'ud*
a thousand years before it happened
also knew that Judas would fulfill it.
Isa al-Masih the Word of Allah said,
"I assure you, one of you will betray me,
one who is eating with me."[3]
Over 500 years before this,
the Word of Allah had enabled the prophet Zechariah
to foresee what God would cause to happen:
Isa would be betrayed
for thirty pieces of silver,[4]
which actually happened
when the priests paid Judas that amount of money
to purchase unwittingly
the Lamb of God who takes away the sins of the world.
"I am going to strike the shepherd
and the sheep will be scattered," Zechariah predicted.
The Word of Allah had even inspired
the prophet Daniel to foresee
not only the death of the Messiah
but also the subsequent destruction of the Temple:
"After this period of 434 years, the Messiah will be killed,
but not for himself,
and the people of the prince that shall come
shall destroy the city and the sanctuary."[5]

---

[1] Acts 1:20; Psalms 69:25
[2] Psalm 41:9
[3] Mark 14:18
[4] Zechariah 11:12
[5] Daniel 9:26

The manner of the Messiah's atoning death
which will not be "for himself"[1]
but for the sins of the whole world
is clearly described in the *Zabur (Psalms)*:
"They pierced my hands and feet."[2]
But Judas had no taste for the Word of God.
He did not treasure these words in his heart.
Isa warned that man cannot live by bread alone
but by every word that proceeds from the mouth of God.
Yet Judas thought he could mock the grace of the Lord
and lie to the Eternal Spirit of Allah.
Judas fooled only himself.
The Word of God could read the traitor's inmost thoughts.
Isa didn't need anyone to tell him what was in a man.
Isa knew what Judas would do.
He allowed him to do it
so that the Scriptures might be fulfilled.
But woe to the man who fulfilled them!

Judas didn't run far.
When all his treachery was over,
he found himself totally alone
and only Satan wanted his detestable company.
So Judas committed suicide.
Now he is in hell.
How do we know?
Because Isa said it would have been better
if he had never been born.
Never having been born
would be like annihilation;
but there is no annihilation in hell,
only conscious eternal anguish,
as it says, "And these shall go away
into everlasting punishment.."[3]
Isa himself warned about the eternal reality of hell
more solemnly and emphatically than anyone.
Therefore, if you want to think like Judas

---

[1] ibid.
[2] Psalm 22:16
[3] Matthew 25:46

and harbor treacherous thoughts that the Word of God is error
and harden your heart's gratitude
against Isa's sacrifice for you to save you from hell,
then there definitely will be room in hell for you with Judas.
But it would be better for you if you had never been born.
The moral judgment of God will require
that every living rebel
will be abandoned forever in the conscious state of his rebellion
as eternal just retribution.

Who could be a bigger fool
than the one who scoffs
at the sacrifical love of the Word of God
who died and rose to speak eternal life into our hearts
and to breathe on us the Eternal Spirit?

This state could have been avoided
had he judged himself and repented of this wickedness,
believing that the Word who is the Judge from Allah
came to die to take the penalty for our crimes.

Who is more worthy of judgment
than the one who rejects the Judge's merciful act
of taking, though himself innocent,
the culprit's penalty of judgment on himself?
Who is more worthy of judgment
than the one who would have the Judge
thus suffer and die in vain?
Who is more worthy of judgment
than the one who would go on, his life unchanged,
wickedly refusing to believe
even after he had heard
of this merciful and loving Judge from Allah?

Who could be a bigger fool than the one who,
being on the side of men and not God,
sells his own soul to eternal torment
for a few fleeting rags in this life?
Judas was an apostle!
He was among those selected for the privilege
of governing the Kingdom of Allah
at the side of the Messiah Himself!

But an upright man can in fact give up
his privileged status before God
and can choose to enjoy for a time the pleasure
of not listening to the true Isa,
of not sharing in the sufferings
that arise because of Isa's words.

(The true Jesus is that one who bled
and died for sin and rose again!).
Any Judas can choose to avoid the trouble that comes
because of the Word of His blood
and of His Judgment
and of His giving of the Spirit.
Any privileged man can betray his own integrity
and can copy a devil like Judas.
Who does this more truly
than the one who has no respect for God's law
and says the Book is now a corrupt pile of errors
and not to be trusted or taken seriously?
Is God's Book in error?
Is it not rather you who are in error,
you who know neither the Scriptures nor the power of God?
Will you judge the Word in error
or will the Word of God judge *you* in error?
Which will it be?
The folly of your judgment of the Word?
Or the judgment of the Word on your folly?

Oh the horror of this betrayal of the Word of God!
The horror of hell is that God allows us
to attain what our wicked hearts demand:
the lie of *al-Dajjal* (Anti-Christ) which we love
rather than the truth of Messiah
which we love to call error.
Judas wanted it this way
and the horror is that God allowed him his way.
Only God can take this treachery out of our minds;
it was there from the time that the first human being
rebelled against the holy commandment.
That spiritual treachery is still there today
when the Word of God is read by skeptical rebels.

Only the Lord can remove this treachery from our hearts.
The Lord did this for Peter,
an apostle who also denied the Lord
and also refused to die with him.
The Lord removed Peter's treacherous unspiritual nature
and gave him a new spirit,
so that he would never deny the Lord again
but would take up his cross
and even be willing to die for the Lord.
Only the Lord can remove this treachery
and He does it when we turn to him.
But if we refuse, note well:
fury grips the Lord when He sees
the wicked treacherously abandoning His Word.
Do you want to call His Word error and make him angry?
Are you stronger than the Lord?

Some declare they have light
but it is in fact a false knower's light,
like the light in the ancient heresies.
And if the light within you is darkness,
how great is that darkness!
These "knowers" in their wicked pride
go beyond what is written
and boast of "knowledge" higher than
the faith once for all delivered to the holy ones.
With brazen tongues and dead-looking eyes
these self-willed souls
refuse the knowledge that could bring them life.
Their arrogance knows no bounds;
like a raging wind that swirls and casts up dirt
wherever it flies,
so their minds rush
to call error the Word
and the Word error.
(Who are you to interpret the true Word,
you without true faith from Allah's Eternal Spirit?)

THE NEED FOR A NEW HUMAN NATURE

From such thinking came
the Primal Lapse:

when the first human ears
were tickled with the taunt,
"Hath God said...?"
It was then that *Shaitan* (Satan),
that ancient Gnostic,[1]
boasted of knowledge higher than
the Word of Allah
and tempted mankind to *islam* (submit) to *his* will
rather than to the will of Allah.
Thus mankind gave up
the true and living Eternal Word
for a death-dealing Satanic caricature—
    a false Word,
    a devilish Word,
    another Message.

It was then that a heart,
made good by God,
turned devilishly perverse.
It was then that humanity,
by presuming it could know good and evil
and find life
by some means other than *islam* (submission)
to the true and living Word of God,
fell.

Yes, humanity fell,
and how great was the fall of it!
So great indeed
that those with fallen minds
unrenewed by the Eternal Spirit
and the personal Word of Allah
are themselves blind to the Fall,
even though their own warped thinking
is part of the Fall's debris!

---

[1] Broadly speaking, a *gnostic* is a heretic who ignores his creator Isa the Word of God and claims for himself a supposedly higher knowledge—the Greek word for knowledge is *gnosis*—leading to life and salvation. See Genesis 2:17; 3:5,22

What more evidence for the Fall do I need
than my own fallen life?
The heart of man is desperately wicked,
who can know it?
For the honest man who looks
within the depths of his soul
will say this:
I fail to carry out the good I know I should do
and I find myself doing the very things I hate.
When I act against my own intention
that means that I have a self that knows the good,
and so the thing behaving wickedly in me
must surely be my fallen nature.
I know of nothing good living in me.
My lower nature is my unspiritual self,
possessing only a faint and fickle wish
to do what is good
but not the effecting will
(only those who are new creations in Isa the saving Word
have the effecting will
with the tender conscience.)[1]
What is the result then?
Instead of doing the right
I want to do,
I carry out the wicked wrong
I do not want.
When I act against my intention, then,
it is not I alone who am the agent,
but the fallen nature
that lodges in me.
Wretched rebel that I am,
who is there to rescue me out of this fallen flesh,[2]
this treacherous will,
this rebel nature doomed to death?
How can I become a true *muslim* (submitter) to Allah

---

[1] I John 5:18-19; 3:21
[2] The term *nafs la-ammara bilso*, meaning "the sin-prone soul" is found in Joseph 12:53, and this is the closest Quranic term for the fallen flesh, which is the unredeemed nature of mankind that can only be changed by the miracle of regeneration and new birth unto eternal life.

and receive a new creation nature?
This is the question of all questions.

THE HARDENED HEART WITHOUT THE NEW CREATION IS SHAMELESS

But some don't even ask the question.
Some people have no sense of shame.
The man of God learned this when,
having helped Ahmad save *his* marriage,
the man of God himself had marital tragedy.
We will call the name of the man of God "Hosea"
though he lived in modern times.

This is a true story.

One day he stood up in the house of God to preach.
But a supernatural word came to him,
not from the words of a paper book,[1]
but from the Eternal Spirit of Allah.
What came to him is best described as supernatural knowledge.
The living Word that spoke to his heart
was as urgent as a shout
and as vivid as a vision.
The man of God saw in this miraculous manifestation
materializing before the eye of his mind
his wife in a bedroom many miles away.
The person he saw with her was in the act
of committing adultery.

The man of God stood before the congregation
and he could not begin the *khutba* (sermon),
because in his spirit he was in the bedroom
horrified at the sight of this evil

---

[1] This gift of the Spirit is still for today—I Cor. 12:8. However, a true instance of supernatural knowledge never contradicts or in any way devalues the closed canon of the infallibly accurate written Word of God. The language used here is not meant to show a superiority of the charismatic power-encounter over against the written Bible, but over against non-canonical or non-Biblical writings.

Allah was showing him.
(When Allah gives supernatural knowledge
He never contradicts or goes beyond
His infallible written Word.)

The next morning the man of God
wanted to make sure this vision was true
and not just his own imagination.
He travelled to the house
and, finding no one home,
was able to examine the bedroom privately.
The evidence left by the careless lovers
(who thought the man of God would have to be preaching
at the hour of their rendezvous
and therefore could not possibly catch them)
showed unmistakably that the vision was from God.

The man of God confronted the adulterous woman.
She had no sense of shame.
"Why should she?" she thought.
No one had caught her in the act,
and as far as the man of God was concerned,
she thought his vision was probably just a lucky guess.

But had not God himself caught her?
Had he not used a gift of His Eternal Spirit,
the gift of supernatural knowledge,
to show the man of God
what only three in the world
—that is, the adulterous woman, her lover, and God—knew?
Had not God himself caught her in the very act of adultery,
a wicked act of treachery worthy of death?

But the woman had no sense of guilt before God.
Allah was very far off to her, *baaeed* (very remote and separate)
and often the thought of God left her cold,
like the thought of her husband.

THE PEOPLE OF THE WORLD, EVEN THE RELIGIOUS PEOPLE,
 ARE LIKE AN ADULTEROUS WIFE

The adulterous wife of the man of God

might speak of God in passionate terms
as she might speak of her husband,
but her rebellious heart was always sneaking off
after that which really excited her.
No, it was no part of her religious experience
to ever feel caught in shame before the believers
or to feel guilty of sin before God.
Her reasoning was that she was no worse than any one else.
Besides, she thought, couldn't she always do good
to counterbalance her sins?
She never thought of herself
as having a "fallen nature."
And since God did not seem close at hand
to catch her in this treacherous state,
    this adulterous nature,
    this unregenerate whorish heart,
she never felt a guilty dissatisfaction
with her own unspiritual self.
Nor did she ever feel a burning need
for a clean, new creation nature.

Just a bit more religion would do the trick, she thought.
For when she was with her co-religionists
involved in religion,
she could see she seemed to be at least
as good as those who did
her same supposedly merit-earning religious rituals.

Some people have no sense of shame.
They do not ask the question,
"Who can rescue me from this rebel nature?"
They do not ask,
"How can I become a *muslim* (true submitter) to Allah
and receive a new creation nature?"
They are like this woman,
without a sense of being caught in shame before a holy God,
a God who finds you guilty in your very nature,
not just in your sins
—a God who wants to give you a new holy nature,
one that has an effecting will not to sin;
with his Eternal Spirit giving you
the tender conscience of His Word.

The Straight Path of the New Creation　　　　　　　　　*51*

But you say, "I am not like her.
   I don't commit adultery.
   I don't need a new nature."
Have you ever looked with lust at another person?
Don't you know that such looks
come out of an adulterous heart?
Don't you know that God wants to give you
a new spiritual heart,
one that recoils in revulsion at even the thought of sin,
a heart where the mind of Allah Himself is mindful?

Stop being satisfied with your unspiritual self
disguised under robe upon robe of religion!
Don't you know that you too must become a new creation?

Those who do supposedly merit-earning religious rituals
without a new creation nature from Allah,
and think they are pleasing Allah,
are going to be eternally surprised.
Somewhere He has called
such religious people "an abomination."[1]
Unless your righteousness exceeds people like this,
you will not enter the Kingdom of Allah. [2]

For God is a covenant-loyal God,
a faithful and a holy husband,
but the people who are not a new creation
and are merely religious
are to Him those who have an adulterous heart worthy of hell.
They have the nature of a rebellious wife that makes God angry.
For the burning lake of hell fire and brimstone is reserved for these:
   those who claim to believe but who are offended when persecution comes,
   those who are untrustworthy in holding forth the true witness,
   those who are morally unclean in any way or detestably idolatrous,

---

[1] Isaiah 1:13
[2] Matthew 5:20

those with murderous hatred in their hearts,
those who are sensually fixated or practice sex disallowed by Allah,
those involved in magic charms, degraded religion or the occult,
those who are covetously idolatrous or consult false prophets,
those who do not live and tell the truth. (Revelation 21:8)

God takes no pleasure in the torment of the wicked in hell,
and neither does a true prophet
take pleasure in the death of the wicked.
Who can preach these things without tears?
Yet they must be proclaimed,
for how can any be saved from destruction
without a new creation nature spoken into existence
by the living and eternal Word of Allah?

Please understand that the intention
is not to demean anyone,
but to awaken everyone and see everyone delivered
from the coming fury and the anguish that is forever.
We treat all people with reverence and humility,
and we discern in them some vestige of the image of Allah,
not entirely faded, even from the vilest.
For a glimmer of the goodness of the God who made him
still shines from every man,
making all accountable when,
even though they hear,
they refuse to obey the Word.

We treat all people with reverence,
knowing that the Word of Allah himself
thought every soul worth dying for
and has ascended to the right hand of God
where He is the universal Leader
of our congregational prayers,
our *Imam* (Leader),
who makes intercession for the elect.
And how can we be irreverent toward one
about whom our *Imam*, Isa the Word of Allah,
may Himself be interceding?

The Straight Path of the New Creation

Oh the depth of the riches
both of the wisdom and power of God!
Our God is a consuming fire!
As His salvation is endless
so is His just judgment of torment for the wicked!

If you feel absolutely no shame or guilt before God,
not just because of the sin you have done,
but because of the sinner you are by nature,
then you may rest assured
that you are like the woman in this true story.

Why?
Because she feels exactly like you,
without shame or guilt before God.
For her, merit-earning religious ritual is enough,
because she has a corrupt mind and counterfeit faith,
having seared the tender conscience
the Eternal Spirit would give her.
She presumptuously thinks she can live any way she wants,
without a new nature,
and be continually forgiven as
she salutes a few religious rules
yet remains in her unregenerate, rebellious state.

Are you going to be like her?
—Not guilty or shameful enough
to feel the need for a new creation nature?

She thinks Allah will be pleased with her when she dies.
But that day will not mean what she thinks.
It will be a day of darkness and not light.
This deluded woman thinks her life is her own
to do with according to a few religious rules
(which she secretly breaks from time to time)
and she's very happy with herself
and with the rules she agrees to go by
and with the life she has made for herself,
with the life she has found for herself.

But whoever finds his life
will lose it;

Whoever loses his life
and receives the gift of a new creation nature
will find his life again
and keep it for eternity.

Does not the very honor of the husband
require that this adulterous woman
should be punished?
Or should she be allowed
to go on like this,
smugly thinking God does not see her,
even when a man of God
supernaturally tells her that God can see her?

Does not such ignorant stubbornness make you angry?
God has given her *years* to repent and reform,
but she has abused His patience and tolerance,
refusing to own up to the fact that His goodness
is meant to lead her to repentance.
She thinks God is like her,
and so she defiantly puts God's honor to the test.
With her brainless lovers and her inexhaustible adulteries,
she continually brings dishonor
not only on her husband's house
but also on her father's household,
and even on the household of God.

She and her lovers are a brood that God detests.
They are one-of-a-kind with the accursed children of Adam.
The first man, Adam, and his wife
were attracted and satanically seduced
by their own wrong desires when they believed Satan's lie
that the Word of Allah is error.
When they hardened their hearts against Allah and His Word,
they gave birth to a breed more wicked than themselves.
When they rebelled against His Word,
deciding they knew more than God,
they fell from the glory of His likeness.
Now the human race,
although it pays lip service to religion,
is steeped in unrighteousness, war, wrangling, murder,
depravity, maliciousness, arrogance, self-seeking,

The Straight Path of the New Creation

vile speech, and treachery of every sort
—a community of snakes coiling around snakes!
And the leaders are the worst vipers in the pit!
They have hardened their hearts against the love of God,
and their wicked pride shuts up all remorse for their sin.
Sin? Their minds are always enterprising in it!
Fierce wolves in sheep's clothing,
the religious teachers
publish empty dreams and lying visions
that lead the Lord's lost sheep astray.
Not content with that,
they persecute the true shepherds
and murderously eat the flesh of the little lambs
and tear off their hoofs.
Don't they know that God loves people?
God wants all people to know who He is
and who they can become as submitters to Him!
Do these sleek religious wolves know God
or even care to know Him?
They do not!

Like Balaam's ass (that donkey prophet),
they see an angel and give a message.
And if even a man supported by a woman declares himself
to be *the* Messianic Prophet,
these wolves will become his fast friends
and sing his praises,
and want to kill anyone
who disagrees with their authority to be his butchers!
These false prophets preach a tinsel word,
an ear-tickling word,
a bloodless word
that cannot save.

Who is more wicked than the unregenerate prophet
who will not tell the way to regeneration?
They themselves will not venture out into the breach,
yet these butchers pour out the blood
of their own people without a qualm
and even dare to do this in the name of God!

Will the adulterous hypocrites who follow them
not be made as guilty and ashamed
as the treacherous hypocrites who lead them?
Does not the very honor of Allah
require that this pretentious brood
all be thrown into hell?
Yes, a rebel prophet with a lying vision
and all the rebels at heart
who love to listen to lies
will burn together.

A darkened race!
We cry out to Allah when in need,
but we forget Him as soon as He answers,
greeting His speedy abundance
with our not-long-in-coming pride.
He shows us great signs and wonders,
but the spiritually dense
are more impressed with themselves.

Be warned, you impotent leaders of the world,
you set of rebels ruling rebels:
submit to the Word of Allah
and kiss His death-conquering feet
or, despite the massive mutiny you mount against Him,
the blast of His anger will be a flame
you can never put out.

For the furious anger of Allah
has been revealed from heaven
against all the ungodliness of men
who hold the truth down
in their unrighteousness.
These enemies of God claim to serve Him,
but in the name of truth and religion
they crucify *al-Haqq* (the Truth) Himself
and, if possible, hold Him down forever
—but it is *not* possible, because Allah himself
has raised His Truth triumphant
over death, hell and murderous false prophets!

Such liars widen the mouth of hell
to gulp those like them down the more,
and so they cause in the land
a famine of hearing the true Word of Allah.
Allah is angry with the whole race of Adam.
He has vowed such accursed children of Adam
to His Word for destruction
and marked them down to His Truth for public execution.

Are you ignorant that Allah decreed
the death and rebirth of the whole human race?
Did you not know that the Word of Allah Himself
brought the decree?
The old race Allah nailed up naked and dying
and the new race He raised up clothed in glory.
The decree of death to the sinful dying race
and decree of life to the glorious holy race
came through the Word of Allah Isa al-Masih!
Did you not know that *al-Haqq* (the Truth)
came as Truth to bear witness to the Truth?
A Roman governor (Pilate) who put Isa (Jesus) on trial
asked him,
"What is Truth?"
This wicked soul did not know it was *he* who was on trial
and it was the whole brood of such as he
that Isa the Word of Allah would doom
in His own sacrificial flesh.

How, then, has God revealed his anger?
God sent His flaming Word
who will one day finally
remove the anguished wicked from His Presence;
God sent His burning, pure and sinless Word
into our fallen and wicked world
in a body as physical as any sinful body,
in order to publicly condemn
our fallen nature in the flesh.
God thus summarily put to death
the race of Adam,
and has been replacing it
with the new creation *ummah* (community)
of the Word of Allah,

as each new believer
hears, believes, repents,
and is spiritually born from above to have a holy nature
like that of Isa the Word of Allah.
For God is not willing that any should perish.
God is holding open the opportunity
for many to die
to their faithless life in Adam's race
and to come alive
to their pure and holy new life
in the race of the Word of Allah.

Why is the death and rebirth of the whole race of Man necessary?
God could not let our sinful will go unpunished.
His honor could not allow it.

His justice demanded punishment
for our wickedness
and his honor demanded death
for our sin against His holiness.

However, God loves the world
and, like a heart-broken husband of an adultress
wooing back his faithless wife,
God by no means wants to destroy His creation.
So with an open palm of heavenly reconciliation
held out in the one hand,
and with a fist of hellish reprisal
threatening in the other,
God comes to this adulterous world
to get her decision:
will she or will she not
let Him make her into a new creation
and take her back honorably,
in covenant faithfulness and loyalty to Him,
her death-deserving sin and its blood debt paid.
He sent the Bridegroom of His Honor, His Word,
to enrobe Himself in our humanity
and to serve the death warrant of Allah
on our sinful race.
This was to save the honor of Allah.

Then His Word came to life again
to vouchsafe Allah's promise to a new forgiven humanity
who would leave their old corrupt minds
and receive the mind of Isa
to be spiritually raised to life with him.
This was to save the honor of believers.

Praise be unto Allah for His Eternal Word Isa!
Then, honorably unburdened of their wicked past,
all those who had longed to obey the Word of God
could be given the gift of a blessed future
and, as new creations, could become true submitters to Allah.
If the honor of Allah
or the honor of your own life before Allah
means anything to you,
you can come today to the kind of godly shame
and righteous sorrow for sin
that leads to salvation.
You can receive the living Word of Allah
through faith by calling out to Him now.
You can become part of His new humanity today.

But you say,
"I have many questions.
You have discussed evil at length;
why does Allah tolerate the wicked at all?
Why are they allowed to prosper?"

Since the present is but a brief preparation
for a more demanding future,
the seeming prosperity of the wicked
is really their curse,
in that he who is muddled by money
is ill-prepared for imminent coming judgment,
and so his "prosperity" seals his doom.

We are just one heart-beat away
from death and eternal judgment.
When we die we will become aware
of standing before the judgment throne
of the eternal Word of Allah—the Word who took the judgment
(by his death in our place)

of those who have faith in him
and forsake all boasting
in dead religious works.
The more wickedness a man does
and the more reward he seems to acquire from it,
the more lulled he is into being caught
in his wicked condition,
which is a state worthy of eternal damnation.

THE MERCY OF THE MESSIAH TOWARD THE UNFAITHFUL

The following true story
illustrates both the justice and the merciful love
of Allah's eternal Word, Isa al-Masih:
"At daybreak Isa appeared in the Temple again;
and all the people came to him,
and he sat down and taught them.
The legalistic teachers and some members of the legalistic sect
brought a woman along who had been caught committing adultery
and making her stand there in the middle they said to Isa,
'Teacher, this woman was caught
in the very act of committing adultery.
Now in the *Taurat* (Torah) Musa has ordered us
to stone women of this kind.
What do you say about her?'
They asked him this as a test,
in order that they might have some charge
to bring against him.
But Isa bent down
and started writing on the ground with his finger.
And as they persisted with their question,
he straightened up and said,
'Let him who is without sin among you
be the first to throw a stone at her.'
Then he bent down and continued writing on the ground.
When they heard this they went away one by one,
beginning with the eldest,
until the last one had gone and Isa was left alone
with the woman standing before him.
Isa again straightened up and said,
'Woman, where are they? Has no one condemned you?'

'No one, sir,' she replied.
'Neither do I condemn you,' said Isa.
'Go and sin no more.' "[1]
The woman in the story knew that she was as good as dead
because two witnessess (the prescribed number)
had caught her in the very act of committing adultery,
of which the Torah's penalty was death.
Isa could have treated her with loathing,
as men all too often act toward women.
Instead, he gave her new life and enabled her not to sin anymore
but to surender to Allah as a New Creation Muslim.
This is God's will for all people, male and female,
for Allah is the merciful giver of new life.

THIS IS THE CONCLUSION OF THE MATTER

In the beginning God
thought
and by His creative Word spoke.
The divine Word called a universe out of nothing.
And by nothing but His Word
are the revolving stars held together.
Of all the created beings,
man alone has a reasonable word,
an utterable word,
a human word
—and a self-seeing spirit.
For humanity is not made in the likeness of an animal,
but in the likeness of Allah
who is Eternal God-with-His-Eternal-Word-and-His-Eternal
Spirit.
He it is who is the true God.

And this one God alone
makes mankind into a new creation
that reflects His glory
because the mankind He makes new
is Man-with-renewed-mind-and-regenerated-spirit.

---

[1] John 8:1-11

We lose the old rebellious selfhood but not the self.
We lose our old independent identity but not our identity.
We are not swallowed up into religious mysticism.
We need no occultist techniques or exercises to approach Allah.
All we need to do is to repent
and bring every thought captive to obey the Word
by yielding to the power of the Eternal Spirit,
so that the mind that was in Isa al-Masih is in us
as we live and speak and act in inner communion with Him.

THE *TARIQA* (WAY) FOR NEW CREATION MUSLIMS

Shaitan (the Devil) is ultimately not able
to overpower a person
who is on the right path.
The beginning of the right path is Allah's living Word,
not a paper book sent down to be worshipped as a fetish
but a living personal Word sent down
that we might have life
and have it more abundantly
through a new and living *tariqa* (way)
found only in Isa's inerrant written words.
Isa said, "I am the *tariqa* (the right path),
the *haqiqah*, (truth)
and the *hayat* (life).
No one comes to the Father
but by me"
(there is no other mediator,
no prophet who can supercede him,
no other name under heaven
whereby we must be saved).

The center of the right path is *Iman* (right Faith),
not in a righteousness of our own
which is of law-keeping and works,
nor of *din* (religious practice) nor *ihsan* (rightdoing),
but that which is through *iman* (faith) in the Word himself,
who comes to us from Allah in the power of the Spirit
both to will and to do his good pleasure,
effecting in us a righteousness which is of God
by faith and not by works,
lest anyone should boast.

The Straight Path of the New Creation

The beginning of the way through is *tawba* (repentance).
This means continually confessing and putting to death
what is prone toward evil within us,
that is, the *qalb* (heart) of a *fasiq* (sinner).
If we say we have no sin,
we deceive ourselves
and the truth is not in us.
If we confess our sins,
he is faithful and just
to forgive our sins,
and to cleanse us
from all unrighteousness.

The inclination of all humanity
—not individually necessitated by Allah
but nevertheless personally and freely chosen
by all Adam's children—
is to sin and therefore to die.
Thus, we must die to self *(al-Junaid fana)*.
We need to put to death in ourselves that which
shares the same sin-prone nature as the old mankind
(we need to die to the *umma* , community, of Adam),
and we must be recreated by the Word of God
(we need to be born anew
into the spiritual *ummah* of the Word of God).

The mystery of the right path
is that the Word of Allah
who is the likeness of the invisible God (Col. 1:15),
became *al-Insan al-Kamil* (the Perfect Man) Isa al-Masih
and died a death to cure the guilt
of the *qalb* (heart) of every *fasiq* (sinner),
so that we can become assured
of our eternal inheritance as new creations,
being daily renewed and perfected.

This mystery is Allah's temporary secret
now made publicly known,
that is, that Isa al-Masih
is the past, present and future pattern of mankind,
and whatever utopia or myth men hope for is unreal
except as the real is seen in Him alive from the dead.

The center of the way through is *inaba* (returning)
to *al-Insan al-Kamil* (the Perfect Man).
To as many as received him (Isa)
to them gave he power to become the heirs of Allah,
and we know that when he shall appear
we shall be like him.

The end of the way through is to submit
in total obedience to Allah
in the *marifah* (knowledge)
of His costly and holy *ishq* (love)
with which He has loved us,
even with the love of a Father.
This is the love God has for us,
the same fatherly love He had for Ibrahim
(whose former name Abram means 'Exalted Father').
Ibrahim himself returned this type of love to Allah
by his willingness to sacrifice to God
his only heir.

The end of the right path
is to daily do the *al-arkan* (right duties)
by the direction and empowering of the Eternal Spirit.
This step is *ubudiyah* (service)
and cannot be done by might
nor by power,
but by His Eternal Spirit.

YOU CAN PRAY THIS PRAYER

"Allah, the merciful and forgiving One,
I confess and agree with your Word
that I have had a sinful will
and have sinned
and need a new will.
I believe the Word of God who is Isa,
is the very expression of your will and can make me pure
as, by the power of your Eternal Spirit,
I am enabled to be like him.
May I never forget the great cost of his blood
to effect the atoning sacrifice
that takes away the penalty for my sins.

The Straight Path of the New Creation

I call on you now and every day
to deliver me from my sins,
which offend you and have caused
the separation between us.
Come into my heart and life,
Isa, the risen Word of Allah,
and fill me with your love
that I might submit to
and follow your commandments
sent down through you
in the *Taurat* and the *Injil*
by the inspiration of the Eternal Spirit.
Lead me on the straight path to the new creation.
On the basis of what Isa al-Masih has done,
I offer this request to you, praise be unto you,
and believe in my heart that through Isa your Word
it is granted. Amen."

New Creation Book for Muslims 3

the Prayer Life of a New Creation Muslim

3

The Prayer Life of a New Creation Muslim

We who are new creation Muslims
have already tasted of the world to come,
and therefore this present world hates us.[1]
In our spiritual beings we have already passed
from spiritual death unto spiritual life,
and *Shaitan* (Satan)
and the evil *jinn* (demons)
and the people of this present world,
because they have not experienced the new creation
through the Word of Allah, who is Isa,
sometimes lash out at us with hatred and persecution.
The spirit that is in them
hates the Spirit that is in us.
But "greater is He (Isa al-Masih) who is in us
than he (*Shaitan*) who is in the world."[2]
And Allah works all things together for good for us.
Therefore, we do not grow weary in well-doing,
> or in praying for our enemies,
> or in cautiously reaching out to them in love,
> or in joyfully suffering for the sake of God's message
> of a servant's love for a needy world.

---

[1] I John 3:13
[2] John 4:4

We need only put on the spiritual armor
of the One who is within us
and we can stand victorious in prayer[1]
as more than conquerors
against our spiritual enemy, Shaitan.
This is spiritual *jihad* [2].
We praise Allah's Word[3]
who loved us when we were yet his enemies,
and who gives us wisdom and power
to show his love in countless ways,
even for our enemies.

PUT ON ARMOR FOR THE BATTLE

In the daily Islamic prayer
one finds the ejaculation:
"I seek refuge from God
from the cursed Satan."
Five times a day,
we who are New Creation Muslims
pause to put on our spiritual armor
and pray in the Spirit.
Since we have "no lasting city"[4]
in this old creation world of sin and death,
the real direction of our prayer
is *not* toward anything in this visible world
but toward God,
who has triumphed over principalities and powers.
We tear down strongholds of *Shaitan*
and war in the Eternal Spirit
in the ministry of intercession,

---

[1] A liturgy should not replace the study and meditation and memorization of the Holy Scriptures. It is offered here to help leaders see that Western worship forms are not indispensible. The Word of God *is* indispensible, however. And this material should not be allowed to become a ritualistic treadmill detour away from personal prayer and Scripture study.
[2] literally, striving in the way of God.
[3] Psalm 56:4,10
[4] Hebrews 13:14

Prayer Life

pointing our prayers toward Isa and toward those in Mecca
as we pray that in Him they may find the True Way.
Isa al-Masih, the Word of Allah, is the true light
of true submitters to the straight path.
Who has Allah appointed but his Word
to be the world-ruler of the new world, the new creation?
And there is no other name under heaven
that has been given among men
by which we must be saved
from the coming wrath.[1]

A discipline which does not earn merit with Allah
but may be an effective means of identifying with Muslims[2]
is to put on the protection of our spiritual armor
in all five daily prayers:
Subh or the morning prayer,
Zuhr or the noon prayer,[3]
'Asr or the afternoon prayer,
Maghrib or the evening prayer,
and *'Ishaa* or the night prayer.
We pray without ceasing,[4]
and we do not, in any case, make of prayer a good deed
calculated to earn God's favor.
We pray to Allah as though He were our gracious Father.
We pray so freely to Him not to win His favor
but because we *have* His favor,

---

[1] Acts 4:12

[2] I Corinthians 9:19-23

[3] Friday is an important "Day of Assembly" for New Creation Muslims. Like those early believers in the *Injil* or the New Testament, we know that the homes of the faithful are acceptable to Allah as places of prayer —see Acts 2:42,46. Friday is important to us because on Friday Isa, performed the great act that has become the foundation for the forgiveness of our sins: on Friday nearly two thousand years ago Isa shed his blood to cover and make expiation or *kaffarah* for our corrupt and fallen human nature. Since it is this noon prayer that is used at the Friday services, the *Zuhr* prayer is given in this section in its entirety. "One person thinks that some days are holier than others, and another thinks them all equal. Let each of them be fully convinced in his own mind." Romans 14:5.

[4] I Thessalonians 5:17

not by *our* good works but by faith in *His* good works
—that He alone has the power to make the wicked righteous
and He alone has turned us from wickedness
to righteousness,
not by our dead religious works but by the works
of Himself and His Eternal Word and His Eternal Spirit
who has made of our old being a New Creation.

THE WUDU (CEREMONIAL WASHING)

In the Muslim manner we wash before we pray.[1]
We have water available[2]
so that believers can prepare themselves before going into the room we have set aside for prayers.
We remove our shoes before going into the room[3]
and we wash our faces and our hands up to the elbows
and our feet up to the ankles.

As we wash we say:
I wash my hands
from the evil things that I did
so that I can do only those things you want me to do, Lord.
I wash my eyes
so that I can see only those things you want me to see.
I wash my ears
so I can hear your voice,
and not the voice of the world.
I wash my feet so that I can walk in your path.[4]

---

[1] When we wash our hands, we remember how Isa al-Masih the Word of Allah performed the ceremonial washing in the upper room—see John 13:3-17. We approach our prayers as it says in Hebrews 10:22 "with our bodies washed with pure water" to remind us that we are clean before God only as we are submerged into the death of Isa, submitting our bodies as Eternal Spirit-washed and dead-to-sin living sacrifices, trusting his death alone to ransom us from the penalty of our old corrupt nature.

[2] *Wudu* means wash.

[3] Exodus 3:5

[4] We do not believe that the water protects us from demons. Nor do we believe any spiritual purpose is served by the precise method in which this washing is carried out nor will we be bound by the ritualistic incantations of

Prayer Life

THE ADHAAN[1]

The *Muaadhdhin* (Caller to prayer) in our messianic mosque services stands to make the announcement to pray[2] and in so doing recites to the congregation our *Al-'Aqeedah* (creed):

Allaahu Akbar, Allaahu Akbar	God is greater, God is greater.
Allaahu Akbar, Allaahu Akbar	God is greater, God is greater.
Ash hadu allaa ilaaha ill Allah,	I bear witness that there is nothing worthy of worship but God.
Ash hadu anna Isa Kalimatu'llah	I bear witness that Isa is the Word of God

---

those who claim knowledge of a traditional and preferred method. It is not the purpose of this section to yoke believers to any system of formalism or ritualism or to detract from a simple, direct prayer life, as Isa taught. Our purpose is to learn to pray in such an Islamic way that Muslims will believe that "we have become all things to all men that we might by all means save some." Moreover, we do believe in demons and that we wrestle against them as believers. We know that we overcome the ruler of all demons, *Shaitan*, by the blood of the Isa—Revelation 12:11. As we apply the water, by faith we cover ourselves with the blood of Isa, the One "that came by water and blood, even Isa al-Masih; not by water only, but by water and blood. And it is the Spirit that beareth witness, because the Spirit is truth."—I John 5:6-7

[1] This is the call to prayer given by the *Muaadhdhin*, who is traditionally an adult male and who stands to make the announcement that brings everyone to form a line behind him on prayer rugs or *sajajid*. Each believer has already been praying and meditating on Scripture before the service begins and no one is talking or looking around. The room is reverently prepared for the prayer service by the prayerful concentration of all the people. Each believer should by faith see the armor of Ephesians 6 in front of him on his prayer carpet as the objects he will use to mark off an area of space or *sutra* within which he is not disturbed by human or demoniacal influences.

[2] In small mosques the *Adhaan* is given by the Imam or prayer leader, though in larger mosques, an official is specially appointed for the purpose. In smaller mosques lacking a minaret the call may be made from the side of the building or from the door or from inside. In any event, a messianic *Muaadhdhin*, focusing his intercessory heart toward the lost millions facing Mecca, stands with his face turned in their direction and, with the points of his thumbs by his ear lobes, recites the messianic formula given here.

hooah yellkee al-ruah al-abadeeah	Who sendeth forth the (Eternal) Spirit[1]
al-moonthick min amr rabbi	Proceeding from the command (*Amr*) of my Lord[2]
Isa al-Masih, Kalimatahoo	Isa the Messiah, His Word[3]
wahfadah kool awlad Ibrahim b'zabahen ahzeemin	The ransom of all Ibrahim's heirs and our momentous sacrifice[4]
wahrahfahahoo Allah eelyihee	Raised to Allah[5]
leeyoonzeerah yeowma althuhlach	As a warning of the day of meeting[6]
innaa annafs laaahnrahoo	That He might put away our
beesooch bell hooah zellah annefs	evil-prone flesh and bring
alchadeem Neenachoonah chahleekah djadeedah	a new creation[7]
leeanna hahteh al-sahllech yahtahbarrar beelman	Even righteousness by faith alone.[8]
Hayya 'alaa Salaah	Hasten to prayer
Hayya 'alal Falaah	Hasten to real success
Qad qaamatis Sallaah	Prayer is ready
Qad qaamatis Sallaah	Prayer is ready.
Allaahu Akbar,	Allah is greater.
Allaahu Akbar	Allah is greater.
Laa ilaaha ill Allah	There is nothing worthy of worship but Allah."[9]

---

[1] Believer 40:15; John 15:26
[2] Banu Israel 17:85; John 20:22
[3] Women 4:171; John 1:1,14
[4] Those Ranged in Ranks. 37:107; I Timothy 2:6; I John 2:2; Galatians 3:29
[5] House of `Imran. 3:55; Acts 1:9
[6] Believer. 40:15; Romans 1:16; John 3:36; Revelation 19:15
[7] Joseph 12:53; Ibrahim 14:19; Romans 6:3; Colossians 2:11-12; II Corinthians 5:17
[8] Adoration 32:12; Romans 3:28
[9] When the Caller to prayer has finished, we are ready to begin the service. The *Imam* may come up at any moment after the first *Adhaan*; As he approaches the three-step riser *Minbar* or pulpit, he faces the worshippers and greets them with "As-Salaamu 'Alaikum" or "Peace be on you." The Imam then sits down facing the believers. The *Imam* gives two messages, one brief and one longer with a free time of worship between them. The sermon or *Khutbah* begins with the formula, *Al hamdu lillaah* ("All praise

A *KHUTBAH* (SERMON) ENTITLED
"GOD'S PLAN FOR THE CHILDREN OF ISRAEL AND ISHMAEL"
—SUITABLE FOR A MESSIANIC ISLAMIC *JUM'AH* OR FRIDAY
SERVICE

"In the name of God, the Compassionate, the Merciful.
Praised be God. Praised be the God who has shown us the way,
the straight path through His Word.
I bear witness that there is nothing worthy of worship
but God.
I bear witness that Isa is the Word of God.
Fear God, O you people,
fear that day,
the Day of Judgment,
when a father will not be able to answer for his son,
nor the son for his father,
when an Imam will not be able to answer for a Muslim,
nor a Rabbi for a Jew.
O you people who have believed,
turn you to God,
as Ibrahim did turn to God.
Truly God is One and forgives all sin through His Word.
Truly we know His Word.
I bear witness that Isa is His Word of forgiveness.
Through Him Allah is merciful,
the forgiver of sins.
Through Him Allah is the most munificent,
and bountiful, the King,
the Holy One, the Most Merciful."

---

is due to Allah") and may occasionally and selectively use the Qur'an as a bridge to illustrate the canonical truth of the authoritative prophetic message given in the Holy Scriptures, provided the leader roots the believers in Scripture alone and does not let them drift away from memorizing and meditating on the only infallible guide for faith and practice. At the conclusion of the sermon, the Imam leads the worshippers in the congregational prayers. It should be noted: all five of the daily prayers have a similar structure and use the same basic prayer postures of standing, bowing, sitting, prostrating, lifting hands, etc. Since the noon prayer is the one also used at the weekly congregational meeting, it is offered here as an example of individual five-times daily devotional prayers useable by messianic Muslims.

(The preacher or *khatib* or *muzakkir* then descends from the pulpit, and sitting on the floor of the place of prayer, offers up a silent prayer. He then again ascends the *minbar* or pulpit, which may be nothing more than a small three step riser in smaller mosques and proceeds.)

"In the name of God, the Compassionate, the Merciful.
Praise be to God."
He who has the living Word of God for His guide
is never lost.
If we have truly died with His Word
and have truly been brought to live again by His Word,
then we truly passed from death to life.
There is a text in the Quran that refers to this:
`Or (take) the similitude
of one who passed
by a hamlet, all in ruins,
to its roofs. He said:
`Oh! how shall Allah
bring it (ever) to life,
after (this) its death?'
Then in that same text (Cow 2:259)
it says:
'Look further at the bones,
how We bring them together,
and clothe them with flesh!'
Many commentators believe this text
is referring to Ezekiel 37:1-10,
which says,
"The hand of the Lord was upon me (Ezekiel),
and carried me out in the Spirit of the Lord,
and set me down in the midst of the valley
which was full of bones,
and caused me to pass by them round about:
and, behold, there were very many in the open valley;
and, lo, they were very dry.
And he (God) said to me,
'Son of man, can these bones live?'
And I answered,
'O Lord God, thou knowest.'
Again he said unto me,

'Prophesy upon these bones,
and say unto them,
O you dry bones,
hear the word of the Lord.
Thus saith the Lord God unto these bones;
Behold, I will cause breath to enter into you,
and you shall live:
And I will lay sinews upon you,
and will bring up flesh upon you,
and cover you with skin,
and put breath in you,
and you shall live;
and you shall know that I am the Lord.'
So I (Ezekiel) prophesied as I was commanded:
and as I prophesied,
there was a noise,
and behold a shaking,
and the bones came together,
bone to his bone.
And when I beheld, lo,
the sinews and the flesh came up upon them,
and the skin covered them above:
but there was no breath in them.
Then said he unto me,
'Prophesy unto the wind,
prophesy, son of man,
and say to the wind,
Thus saith the Lord God;
Come from the four winds, O breath,
and breathe upon these slain,
that they may live.'
So I prophesied as he (God) commanded me,
and the breath came into them,
and they lived,
and stood up upon their feet,
an exceeding great army."

What is this passage talking about?
Is there somewhere a great army
of those who were once dead
but are now being brought to life again?
Are we who are Muslims included or excluded

from that prophesied army?

We Muslims are always asking questions like this.
We always wonder if God is including us.
The most pressing problem we Muslims have
is our spiritual identity.
The solution to that identity problem
has been given to us in the ancient past
through Ibrahim and Ishmael.

But many anti-Muslim teachers and preachers
use the Bible to teach political interpretations
about the promise of the land to Ibrahim
and negative interpretations about Ishmael.
So many Muslims ask,
"Why is it asserted that Allah loves the Jews
as his chosen people more than he loves us Muslims?
Why do so many want to twist the Scriptures
to make us feel rejected?"
But if we begin with the *Taurat*,
B'raisheet (Genesis) chapter 15,
we return to the cornerstone of our faith
as new creation submitters to Allah
and that cornerstone is Ibrahim.
It says, "Ibrahim believed God,"
and consequently it says that it was credited to him
that he became a righteous submitter to the true path.

THE GOD OF ISHMAEL BE PRAISED

In Genesis chapter 16:10
we see that God had a special plan for Ishmael
and his descendants.
In the Scriptures,
the Angel of the Lord appears only
when God has a special plan;
and in 16:10 Ishmael's mother, Hagar,
is told by the angel of the Lord,
"I will so increase your descendants
that they will be too numerous to count."
The original language of 16:12 is often mistranslated.
The actual words are *"PEH-REH AH-DAM,"*

Prayer Life

or "Man (that will live in the) wild."

The last part of 16:12
says that Ishmael will live
"in hostility toward all his brothers."
The reference to Ishmael (the father of the Arab peoples)
and to his hostility "toward all his brothers"
(referring to Isaac, the father of Israel)
is a prophecy very much fulfilled today in the Middle East.

In Genesis 21 God acts to save Ishmael
and his mother,
just as God is saving many Muslims today.

21:19 says "Then God opened her (Hagar's) eyes
and she saw a well of water."
Today God is opening the eyes of many of Ishmael's descendents
and they are coming to the Word of Allah who said,
"If any man thirst,
let him come to me and drink."

Unfortunately, the sons
of those feuding brothers Ishamel and Isaac
have forgotten that their fathers wept together
when they buried their father Ibrahim,
as it says,
"in the cave of Machpelah near Mamre" (Genesis 25:9).

In Isaiah 42:10-12
we see another prophecy,
that the sons of Ishmael (Kedar—see Genesis 25:13)
will come back to God and will
"proclaim his praise in the islands."
We believe this refers to the messianic Islamic *du`at*,
those new creation muslim missionaries
who will be sent out to make the call,
the invitation to submit to Allah
and His Word Isa our Deliverer (*`Asim*).

Again, look at Isaiah 60:7:
"All the flocks of Kedar shall be gathered

together unto thee,
the rams of Nebaioth shall minister unto thee:
they shall come up with acceptance on mine altar,
and I will glorify the house of my glory."

How much clearer can God make it
that a revival is coming among the Muslims?

In Acts 2:9-11 we see much of the modern Muslim world
represented when the Injil was first proclaimed
at *al-Kuds* (Jerusalem);
notice the text lists "the Arabs,"
it lists "Mesopotamia" (Syria and Iraq),
"Libya," "Parthians and Medians"
(part of Kuwait and the Kurdish)
—all sons of Ishmael who are among those
that will come in the last days
as new creations to glorify God.
God has a plan of salvation for them
and wants them to be saved
from his own holy hostility against unholiness
just as he wants Jew and non-Jew to be saved
from the murderous hostility that is between them.

IN THE NEW CREATION, WE LIVE TOGETHER IN PEACE

That hostility has been put to death (Ephesians 2:16)
by the Word who broke down all hostility
in his body on the tree of hostility
when he rose from the dead
to assure us of our triumph with him over all hostility
and our deliverance from the holy hostility of God.

The hostility between Jews and Muslims
over the land of Israel is displeasing to God.
In his Word, God rebukes those who fight
and kill each other over the land.
God says, "The land shall not be sold forever:
for the land is *mine*;
for you are *strangers* and *aliens* with me." (Lev.25:23)
The main point is that any land belongs to
the God of creation.

We are all ephemeral dying aliens here,
on a pilgrimage and under probation and testing
to see if we will submit to the love of God
as revealed by His Word Isa in the book Isa inspired.

Those Jews who hate Muslims also hate the Holy God
whose word promises He will save Muslims in the last days.
Those Muslims who hate Jews also hate the Holy God
whose Word promises He will breathe spiritual life
into these dead bones in the last days.
And, more than that, they hate the God
who promises these bones will be resurrected physically
on the land of Ibrahim
just as they will one day be resurrected spiritually
in the true faith of Ibrahim.

The Jew who hates the Muslim
and the Muslim who hates the Jew
hate the God of their common father Ibrahim
for the Muslim and the Jew are brothers.
If one kills the other over the land of Ibrahim,
they are not gaining any ground with God.
Both push each other into hell,
and who is the better for all their wars?

But what does the Scripture say?
"Whoever hateth his brother is a murderer:
and you know that no murderer
has eternal life abiding in him!" (I John 3:15)
You who say that you are a Jew
(and are not because you hate your brother Muslim),
repent or there is no eternal life abiding in you!
You who say that you are a Muslim
(and are not because you hate your brother Jew),
repent or there is no eternal life abiding in you!

"If a Muslim or Jew says, 'I love God,'
and hateth his brother,
he is a liar:
for he that loveth not his brother
whom he hath seen,
how can he love God

whom he hath not seen?" (I John 4:20)

THE IQAAMAH

The word *Iqaamah* means "causing to stand."[1]

Allaahu Akbar, Allaahu Akbar	Allah is greater, Allah is greater
Ash hadu allaa ilaaha ill Allah	I bear witness that there is nothing worthy of worship but God
Ash hadu anna Isa Kalimatu'llah	I bear witness that Isa is the Word of God
Hayya 'alaa Salaah	Hasten to prayer
Hayya 'alal Falaah	Hasten to real success
Qad qaamatis Salaah	Prayer is ready
Qad qaamatis Salaah	Prayer is ready
Allaahu Akbar, Allaahu Akbar	God is greater, God is greater
Laa ilaaha ill Allah	There is nothing worthy of worship but God.[2]
Ash hadu allaa ilaaha ill Allah	I bear witness that there is nothing worthy of worship but Allah
Ash hadu anna Isa Kalimatu'llah	I bear witness that Isa is the Word of God
Hooah yellkee al-ruah al-abadeeah	Who sendeth forth the (Eternal) Spirit[3]
al-moonthick min amr rabbi	Proceeding from the command (*Amr*) of my Lord[4]
Isa al-Masih, Kalimatahoo	Isa the Messiah, His Word[5]
wahfadah keel awlad Ibrahim	The ransom of all Ibrahim's heirs

---

[1]This is the second call to the prayers or salat which is pronounced by the *Muaadhdhin*, who may be the same person as the *Imam* and the *Imam* is normally the one who gives the sermon. This second call gives the moment when the congregational prayers begin. At this point we stand for prayer and consciously make the intention or *niyyah* to focus with the eye of our spirit upon Isa the Word of Allah who promised "Truly, truly, I say to you, if you shall ask the Father for anything in my name, He will give it to you." See John 16:23.

[2]As the *Muaadhdhin* completes this second call to prayer, the believer is standing, his hands above his shoulders, his finger tips parallel to his ears, as it says "I will therefore that men pray everywhere, lifting up holy hands, without wrath or disputing."—see I Timothy 2:8.

[3]Believer 40:15; John 15:26

[4]Banu Israel 17:85; John 20:22

[5]Women 4:171; John 1:1,14

Prayer Life

b'zabahen ahzeemin	and our momentous sacrifice[1]
wahrahfahahoo Allah eelyihee	Raised to Allah[2]
leeyoonzeerah yeowma althuhlach	As a warning of the day of meeting[3]
innaa annafs laaahnrahoo	That He might put away our
beesooch bell hooah zellah annefs	evil-prone flesh and bring
alchadeem Neenachoonah	a new creation[4]
chahleekah djadeedah	
Leeanna hahteh al-sahllech	Even righteousness by faith alone.[5]
yahtahbarrar beel-man	
Allahu Akbar	Allah is greater[6]
Subhaanakallaahumma	Glory be to You O Allah
wa bihamdik,	and Yours is the praise
wa tabaarakas muka	and blessed is Your Name
wa ta'aalaa	and exalted is Your Majesty
jadduka wa laa ilaaha ghairuk	and there is no deity besides you.
A'uudh billaahi minash	I seek the refuge of Allah
fromshaitaanir Rajeem.	Satan, the accursed.[7]

---

[1] Those Ranged in Ranks. 37:107; I Timothy 2:6; I John 2:2; Galatians 3:29

[2] House of `Imran. 3:55; Acts 1:9

[3] Believer. 40:15; Romans 1:16; John 3:36; Revelation 19:15

[4] Joseph 12:53; Ibrahim 14:19; Romans 6:3; Colossians 2:11-12; II Corinthians 5:17

[5] Adoration 32:12; Romans 3:28

[6] The hands are raised to the shoulders as we praise the one true God self-revealed as God and His Word and His Eternal Spirit. Then placing the hands between the chest and the navel, with the palm of the right hand over the left, and the wrist of the left hand gripped by the right hand, we grasp the breastplate of righteousness, the most important part of our armor. "Above all guard your heart with all diligence; for out of it are the issues of life."—see Proverbs 4:23. If you "believe in your heart that God raised him—Isa—from the dead, you shall be saved. For with the heart man believes unto righteousness"—see Romans 10:9-10. Meditating on this verse, we realize that the World-Judge is alive to judge all men, and that if we believe this with our heart, "every man that hath this hope in Him purifieth himself, even as He—Isa—is pure." see I John 3:3

[7] As we say this we remember that Isa al-Masih, the glorious Word of Allah, taught us to pray to Allah, "Lead us not into temptation but deliver us from the Evil One."—see Matthew 6:13. Then the risen and victorious Word of Allah spoke through the Apostolic author of Ephesians that we must put on the armor of God "always" see Ephesians 6:18—in order to

AL-FAATIHAH

The first chapter of the Qur'an is a prayer.[1]

Bismillaahir Rahmaanir Raheem	In the name of Allah, Most Gracious, Most merciful,
Al hamdu lillaahi rabbil 'aalameen	Praise be to Allah, the Cherisher and Sustainer of the worlds.
Ar Rahamaanir Raheem	Most Gracious, Most Merciful.
Maaliki yaumid Deen	Master of the Day of Judgment.
Iyyaaka na'abudu wa Iyyaaka nasta'een	Thee do we worship, and Thine aid we look for.
Ihdinas Siraatal mustaqeem	Show us the straight way.
Siraatal ladheen an 'amta 'alaihim	The way of those on whom Thou has bestowed Thy Grace,
ghairil maghduubi 'alaihim walad Daalleen. Aameen.	those whose portion is not wrath, and who go not astray. Amen.[2]
Walou tarah	If only thou couldst see[3]

---

stand our ground against the Devil so that we may stand blameless before the Son of Man—see Luke 21:36. Therefore, five times a day is not any too frequent for submitters to Allah to watch and pray as heavy-armed prayer warriors.

[1] This is the opening chapter of the Qur'an and is recited as a prayer, with this in mind: Allah has designated His Word—Isa—to be "Master of the Day of Judgment"—see Daniel 7:13-14; Matthew 25:31-46.

[2] At the end of the recitation of *Al-Faatihah*, it is traditional for the believers to say Aameen or Amen either aloud in a loud prayer or silently in a silent prayer.

[3] An optional portion of the Quran is traditionally recited at this point. Adoration 32:12 is selected here because it illustrates what it means to enter into the death of Isa. If you could leave this world and see the lake of fire where the unbelievers in Isa will be thrown, you would not return the same person. The wickedness of this world would not have the same power over you, because part of you would still be on the other side gazing at the awesome lake of fire. You would be dead to sin and you would not need all kinds of religious rules to remind you to be holy. Realizing that there are only two alternatives in life, either to be baptized into the eternal torment of the lake of fire or to be baptized by faith into the death of Isa, you would come back a believer led by the Eternal Spirit and you would henceforth deal with this wicked world like a dead man, dealing with it as though you had no dealings with it—see I Corinthians 7:29-31.

Prayer Life

is almooshreemoon	when the guilty ones
nakkesoo r'oosahhom	will bend low their heads
eindah rabbahom	before their Lord, (saying:)
Rabbanah Ahbsahranah	"Our Lord! We have seen
wehsameeaohnah	and we have heard:
Feharzahonah	Now then send us back
nahahmeeloo	(to the world): we will
sahlayhahn innah	work righteousness: for we
moochnenoon	do indeed (now) believe."[1]
Subhaana rabbiyah 'Azeem	Glory to my Lord the Great
Subhaana rabbiyal 'Azeem	Glory to my Lord the Great
Subhaana rabbiyal 'Azeem	Glory to my Lord the Great[2]
Sami'allaahu liman hamidah	Allah listens to him who praises Him.[3]
Rabbanaa lakal hamd	Our Lord, to You is due all praise.
Allaahu Akbar	Allah is greater[4]

---

[1] At the end of this part of the prayer, the messianic believer changes to the bowing position called *Rukuu'u* by saying *Allaahu Akbar* or "Allah is greatest." Still standing, the believer bends forward from the torso and, with the hands supporting the weight of his upper body at the knees, he remains standing in this bowing position as he recites the prayers. However, with his hands on his knees, he is aware of the belt of truth, which holds the sword of the Spirit, the Word of God, the only measuring standard of authoritative prophecy and inerrant words "that are able to make you wise unto salvation through faith which is in Isa al-Masih."—see II Timothy 3:15. As the believer feels the blood rushing to his head, he remembers the helmet of salvation which brings "every thought captive to obey al-Masih."—see II Corinthians 10:5. We look neither to the left or to the right, but straight ahead to Isa who is alone the author and finisher of our faith—see Hebrews 12:2.

[2] As one resumes the upright standing position called *Raf'u*, one takes the shield of faith which is able to quench like water every fiery dart from Satan that would otherwise accuse us or discourage us. Then, wrapping ourselves in a garment of praise we exchange the spirit of heaviness—see Isaiah 61:3—for the joy of the Lord, which is our strength.

[3] Unconfessed sin can hinder our prayers. Yet we must remember that even when we were enemies of God, the Messiah made his sacrifice of love for the ungodly. Romans 5:7-11

[4] Now one changes to the position of prostration called *Sujuud*, with the toes of both feet, both knees, both hands, and the forehead touching the

Subhaana rabbiyal a'Alaa	Glory to my Lord, the Most High
Subhaana rabbiyal a'Alaa	Glory to my Lord, the Most High
Subhaana rabbiyal a'Alaa	Glory to my Lord, the Most High
Allaahu Akbar	Allah is greater[1]
Allaahu Akbar	Allah is greater[2]
Subhaana rabbiyal a'Alaa	Glory to my Lord, the Most High
Subhaana rabbiyal a'Alaa	Glory to my Lord, the Most High
Subhaana rabbiyal a'Alaa	Glory to my Lord, the Most High[3]
Allaahu Akbar[4]	God is greater.
Bismillaahir Rahmaanir Raheem	In the name of Allah, Most Gracious, Most merciful,
Al hamdu lillaahi rabbil 'aalameen	Praise be to Allah, the Cherisher and Sustainer of the worlds.
Ar Rahamaanir Raheem	Most Gracious, Most Merciful.
Maaliki yaumid Deen	Master of the Day of Judgment.
Iyyaaka na'abudu	Thee do we worship,

---

ground, with the hands kept apart from one's sides. Such was the manner in which Moses, Daniel and other prophets often prayed before God. Here we put on our feet the boots that equip us to go and share the Good News of how to have peace with Allah through the punishment His Word Isa endured to freely provide for our just acquittal and forgiveness. As our toes press into the prayer carpet, we realize that the only reason our feet are on this earth is so that we can lead the Lord's chosen people to eternal life.

[1] Now the believer changes to a sitting position on the carpet. This position is called *Juluus*. The right foot is upright but the left foot is placed flat on the ground so it can be set on.

[2] Having sat for a very short while, one now prostrates a second time, remembering the Ephesians 6:15 boots that equip us to go and share how to walk in peace with Allah.

[3] This completes a *raka'ah*, and each subsequent one has this basic structure. Since we are messianic believers, we can pray in the Spirit in these positions and not be bound by specific words or forms in any iron-clad way. However, the basic prayer postures and the structure of the prayer's beginning and end as well as the five times a day regularity are all aspects which we can use with great spiritual profit. What believer is there who is so mature that he doesn't need to remind himself at least five times a day that he is in warfare with the powers of evil?

[4] One begins the second *raka'ah*, each of which is the repeatable unit of prayer containing all the various postures, by resuming the standing posture and reciting once again the first chapter of the Qur'an, *Al-Faatihah*.

Prayer Life

wa Iyyaaka nasta'een	and Thine aid we look for.
Ihdinas Siraatal mustaqeem	Show us the straight way.
Siraatal ladheen an 'amta 'alaihim	The way of those on whom Thou has bestowed Thy Grace,
ghairil maghduubi 'alaihim	those whose portion is not wrath,
walad Daalleen. Aameen.	and who go not astray. Amen.[1]
Taaahlleem al-Kitab al-Muqaddas lehinahoo min al-Kitab nitaahlem	Search the scriptures;[2] for in them ye think ye have eternal life:
ahn al-hiyah al-abadeeyawelkeetab yeshhadoo ahnee	and it is these that bear witness of Me.[3]
Al-simah welahreet tezoolan wekelammmee lan yahzool	Heaven and earth will pass away, but my words will not pass away.[4]
Allahu Akbar[5]	God is greater.
Subhaana rabbiyal 'Azeem	Glory to my Lord, the Great
Subhaana rabbiyal 'Azeem	Glory to my Lord, the Great
Subhaana rabbiyal 'Azeem	Glory to my Lord, the Great
Sami'allaahu liman hamidah[6]	Allah listens to him who praises Him.
Rabbanaa lakal hamd	Our Lord to You is due all praise
Allaahu Akbar[7]	Allah is greater.

---

[1] At the end of the recitation of *Al-Faatihah*, it is traditional for the believers to say *Aameen* or Amen either aloud in a loud prayer or silently in a silent prayer

[2] In this next section we recite from the Holy and Inerrant Word of God, the only authoritative measuring standard of true prophecy.

[3] John 5:39

[4] Mark 13:31

[5] Following the Scripture recitation, one changes to the bowing posture called *Rukuu'u* and concentrates not only on the helmet of salvation that keeps our meditations and the words of our mouth acceptable to Allah but also on the belt of truth that holds our life together.

[6] One resumes the upright standing posture called *Rafu* and concentrates on the shield of faith that allows us by the power of the love of Isa al-Masih to bear and believe and hope and endure despite circumstances—see I Corinthians 13:7.

[7] One changes to the position of prostration called *Sujuud*, and intercedes for wisdom on how to wear those Ephesians 6:15 shoes to go to lost souls as

Subhaana rabbiyal a'Alaa	Glory to my Lord, the most High
Subhaana rabbiyal a'Alaa	Glory to my Lord, the most High
Subhaana rabbiyal a'Alaa	Glory to my Lord, the most High
Allaahu Akbar[1]	Allah is greater.[2]
Subhaana rabbiyal a'Alaa	Glory to my Lord, the Most High
Subhaana rabbiyal a'Alaa	Glory to my Lord, the Most High
Subhaana rabbiyal a'Alaa	Glory to my Lord, the Most High
Allaahu Akbar[3]	Allah is greater.
At Tahiyyaatu lillaahi was Salawaatu wat tayyi baatu	All services rendered by words and bodily actions and sacrifice of wealth are due to Allah.
Ash hadu allaa ilaaha illallaah	I bear witness that there is nothing worthy of worship but God.
Ash hadu anna Isa Kalimatu'llah	I bear witness that Isa is the Word of God
Hooah yellkee al-ruah al-abadeeah	Who sendeth forth the (Eternal) Spirit[4]
al-moonthick min amr rabbi	Proceeding from the command (*Amr*) of my Lord[5]
Isa al-Masih, Kalimatahoo, wahfadah kool awlad Ibrahim b'zabahen ahzeemin	Isa the Messiah, His Word[6] The ransom of all Ibrahim's heirs and our momentous sacrifice[7]

God opens a door of utterance so that we can speak the mystery of al-Masih and make the Good News manifestly clear as we ought to speak—see Colossians 4:3-4

[1] One changes to a sitting position on the carpet. This position is called *Juluus*. The right foot is upright but the left foot is placed flat on the ground so it can be sat on.

[2] One prostrates a second time.

[3] One changes to a sitting posture or *Juluus* with the left hand on the left thigh, and the right hand on the right thigh, with the three fingers locked up while the thumb is on the middle finger and the index finger is pointed. Thus I point my whole being to meditate on the inerrant faith once for all delivered to the saints.

[4] Believer 40:15; John 15:26

[5] Banu Israel 17:85; John 20:22

[6] Women 4:171; John 1:1,14

[7] Those Ranged in Ranks. 37:107; I Timothy 2:6; I John 2:2; Galatians 3:29

Prayer Life

wahrahfahahoo Allah eelyihee
leeyoonzeerah yeowma althuhlach
innaa annafs laaahnrahoo
beesooch bell hooah zellah annefs
alchadeem leenachoonah
chahleekah djadeedah
leeanna hahteh al-sahllech
yahtahbarrar beelman

Allaahu Akbar[5]
Bismillaahir Rahmaanir Raheem

Al hamdu lillaahi
rabbil 'aalameen

Ar Rahamaanir Raheem
Maaliki yaumid Deen
Iyyaaka na'abudu
wa Iyyaaka nasta'een
Ihdinas Siraatal mustaqeem
Siraatal ladheen an 'amta 'alaihim

ghairil maghduubi 'alaihim
walad Daalleen. Aameen.

Raised to Allah[1]
As a warning of the day of meeting[2]
That He might put away our
evil-prone flesh and bring
a new creation[3]

Even righteousness by faith alone.[4]

God is greater.
In the name of Allah,
Most Gracious, Most merciful,
Praise be to Allah,
the Cherisher
and Sustainer of the worlds.
Most Gracious, Most Merciful.
Master of the Day of Judgment.
Thee do we worship,
and Thine aid we look for.
Show us the straight way.
The way of those on whom Thou
has bestowed Thy Grace,
those whose portion is not wrath,
and who go not astray. Amen.[6]

---

[1]House of `Imran. 3:55; Acts 1:9
[2]Believer. 40:15; Romans 1:16; John 3:36; Revelation 19:15
[3]Joseph 12:53; Ibrahim 14:19; Romans 6:3; Colossians 2:11-12; II Corinthians 5:17
[4]Adoration 32:12; Romans 3:28
[5]One resumes the standing position or *Qiyaam* to begin the third *raka'ah* while meditating on the breastplate of righteousness, not my own righteousness based on my works, but the gift of righteous, eternal life, not by good deeds so that no one can boast but by faith, and this itself is not from ourselves—it is a gift of God. Who can make himself a new creation? What do we have or what have we become that is from ourselves? It is all of grace, all a gift, and we have nothing to offer but a scrap of gratitude (Philippians 3:9; Ephesians 2:8-9; I Corinthians 4:7.)
[6]At the end of the recitation of *Al-Faatihah*, it is traditional for the believers to say Aameen or Amen either aloud in a loud prayer or silently in a silent prayer

Allaahu Akbar[1]	Allah is the greater.
Subhaana rabbiyal 'Azeem	Glory to my Lord, the Great
Subhaana rabbiyal 'Azeem	Glory to my Lord, the Great
Subhaana rabbiyal 'Azeem	Glory to my Lord, the Great
Sami'allaahu liman hamidah	Allah listens to him who praise Him
Rabbana lakal hamd	Our Lord to You is due all praise
Allaahu Akbar[2]	Allah is the greater.
Subhanna rabbiyal a'Alaa	Glory to my Lord, the Most High
Subhanna rabbiyal a'Alaa	Glory to my Lord, the Most High
Subhanna rabbiyal a'Alaa	Glory to my Lord, the Most High
Allaahu Akbar[3]	Allah is the greater.[4]
Allaahu Akbar[5]	Allah is the greater.
Subhaana rabbiyal a'Alaa	Glory to my Lord, the Most High
Subhaana rabbiyal a'Alaa	Glory to my Lord, the Most High
Subhaana rabbiyal a'Alaa	Glory to my Lord, the Most High[6]
Bismillaahir Rahmaanir Raheem	In the name of Allah, Most Gracious, Most merciful,
Al hamdu lillaahi rabbil 'aalameen	Praise be to Allah, the Cherisher and Sustainer of the worlds.

---

[1] One now changes to the bowing position called *Rukuu'uk*, concentrating again on the belt of truth and the helmet of salvation, asking God to renew our mind with the humble mind of Isa al-Masih, the way, the truth, and the life. Philippians 2:5-11; John 14:6.

[2] One changes to the position of prostration or *Sujuud* and concentrates on the Ephesians 6:15 boots again, and the only purpose we have to go anywhere, which is to be a light in darkness for Isa al-Masih—see Matthew 5:14.

[3] One changes to the sitting position or *Juluus*.

[4] One sits in this position a very short time.

[5] One prostrates a second time, focusing on thebare feet of Isa al-Masih, the spikes driven through them and the blood, and his commission to us to go—see Matthew 28:19, wearing the shoes of the preparation and readiness to proclaim in word and deed the Good News of how to have peace with Allah—See Ephesians 6:15.

[6] This completes the third *raka'ah*. There is one more left to finish the noon prayer which is also the congregational weekly prayer. It has four *raka'aats*. The morning prayer or Subh only has two, the afternoon prayer or'Asr has four, the evening prayer or *Maghrib* has three, and the *'Ishaa* (night prayer) has four.

Prayer Life

Ar Rahamaanir Raheem	Most Gracious, Most Merciful.
Maaliki yaumid Deen	Master of the Day of Judgment.
Iyyaaka na'abudu	Thee do we worship,
wa Iyyaaka nasta'een	and Thine aid we look for.
Ihdinas Siraatal mustaqeem	Show us the straight way.
Siraatal ladheen an 'amta 'alaihim	The way of those on whom Thou has bestowed Thy Grace,
ghairil maghduubi 'alaihim	those whose portion is not wrath,
walad Daalleen. Aameen.	and who go not astray. Amen.[1]
Allaahu Akbar.	Allah is the greater.
Subhaana rabbiyal 'Azeem	Glory to my Lord, the Great
Subhaana rabbiyal 'Azeem	Glory to my Lord, the Great
Subhaana rabbiyal 'Azeem	Glory to my Lord, the Great
Sami'allaahu liman hamidah Him	Allah listens to him who praises
Rabbana lakal hamd	Our Lord to You is due all praise
Allaahu Akbar[2]	Allah is the greater.
Subhanna rabbiyal a'Alaa	Glory to my Lord, the Most High
Subhanna rabbiyal a'Alaa	Glory to my Lord, the Most High
Subhanna rabbiyal a'Alaa	Glory to my Lord, the Most High
Allaahu Akbar[3]	Allah is the greater.[4]
Allaahu Akbar[5]	Allah is the greater.
Subhaana rabbiyal a'Alaa	Glory to my Lord, the Most High
Subhaana rabbiyal a'Alaa	Glory to my Lord, the Most High
Subhaana rabbiyah a'Alaa	Glory to my Lord, the Most High
Allaahu Akbar[6]	Allah is the greater.
At Tahiyyaatu lillaahi was Salawaatu wat tayyi baatu	All services rendered by words and bodily actions and sacrifice of wealth are due to Allah.

---

[1] At the end of the recitation of *Al-Faatihah,* it is traditional for the believers to say *Aameen* or Amen either aloud in a loud prayer or silently in a silent prayer.

[2] One changes to the position of prostration or *Sujuud,* focusing again on the reason for our existence—"To me to live is al-Masih!"—see Philippians 1:21.

[3] One changes to the sitting position or *Juluus.*

[4] One sits in this position a very short time.

[5] One prostrates a second time.

[6] Now one changes to the sitting posture or *Juluus.*

Ash hadu allaa ilaaha illallaah	I bear witness that there is nothing worthy of worship but God.
Ash hadu anna Isa Kalimatu'llah	I bear witness that Isa is the Word of God
Hooah yellkee al-ruah al-abadeeah	Who sendeth forth the (Eternal) Spirit[1]
al-moonthick min amr rabbi	Proceeding from the command (*Amr*) of my Lord[2]
Isa al-Masih, Kalimatahoo, wahfadah kool awlad Ibrahim b'zabahen ahzeemin	Isa the Messiah, His Word[3] The ransom of all Ibrahim's heirs and our momentous sacrifice[4]
wahrahfahahoo Allah eelyihee leeyoonzeerah yeowma althuhlach	Raised to Allah[5] As a warning of the day of meeting[6]
innaa annafs laaahnrahoo beesooch bell hooah zellah annefs alchadeem Neenachoonah chahleekah djadeedah	That He might put away our evil-prone flesh and bring a new creation[7]
leeanna hahteh al-sahllech	Even righteousness by faith alone.[8]
As Salaamu 'Alaikum wa rahmatullaah	May Allah's peace be upon you and His mercy[9]
As Salaamu 'Alaikum wa rahmatullaah	May Allah's peace be upon you and His mercy[10]

---

[1] Believer 40:15; John 15:26
[2] Banu Israel 17:85; John 20:22
[3] Women 4:171; John 1:1,14
[4] Those Ranged in Ranks. 37:107; I Timothy 2:6; I John 2:2; Galatians 3:29
[5] House of `Imran. 3:55; Acts 1:9
[6] Believer. 40:15; Romans 1:16; John 3:36; Revelation 19:15
[7] Joseph 12:53; Ibrahim 14:19; Romans 6:3; Colossians 2:11-12; II Corinthians 5:17
[8] Adoration 32:12; Romans 3:28
[9] Turning the face to the right side, blessing and interceding for those on the right.
[10] Turning the face to the left side, blessing and interceding for those on the left. Here the new creation Muslims can stand for dismissal prayer with an opportunity for laying on of hands, prayer for the sick, prayer for spiritual

Hebrews 11:13-16 and 13:14 speak of the believer's pilgrimage. The next book will point you onward toward that pilgrimage, which begins with your confession of faith in your prayers.

---

anointing, or invitation to repent and to receive Isa as the saving Word of Allah whose blood makes *kaffarah* or atonement, expiation for the soul. After this there can be a recess to home groups or to another room for the love feast and/or the Id al-Adha Supper of Isa.

New Creation Book for Muslims 4
the New Creation Confession

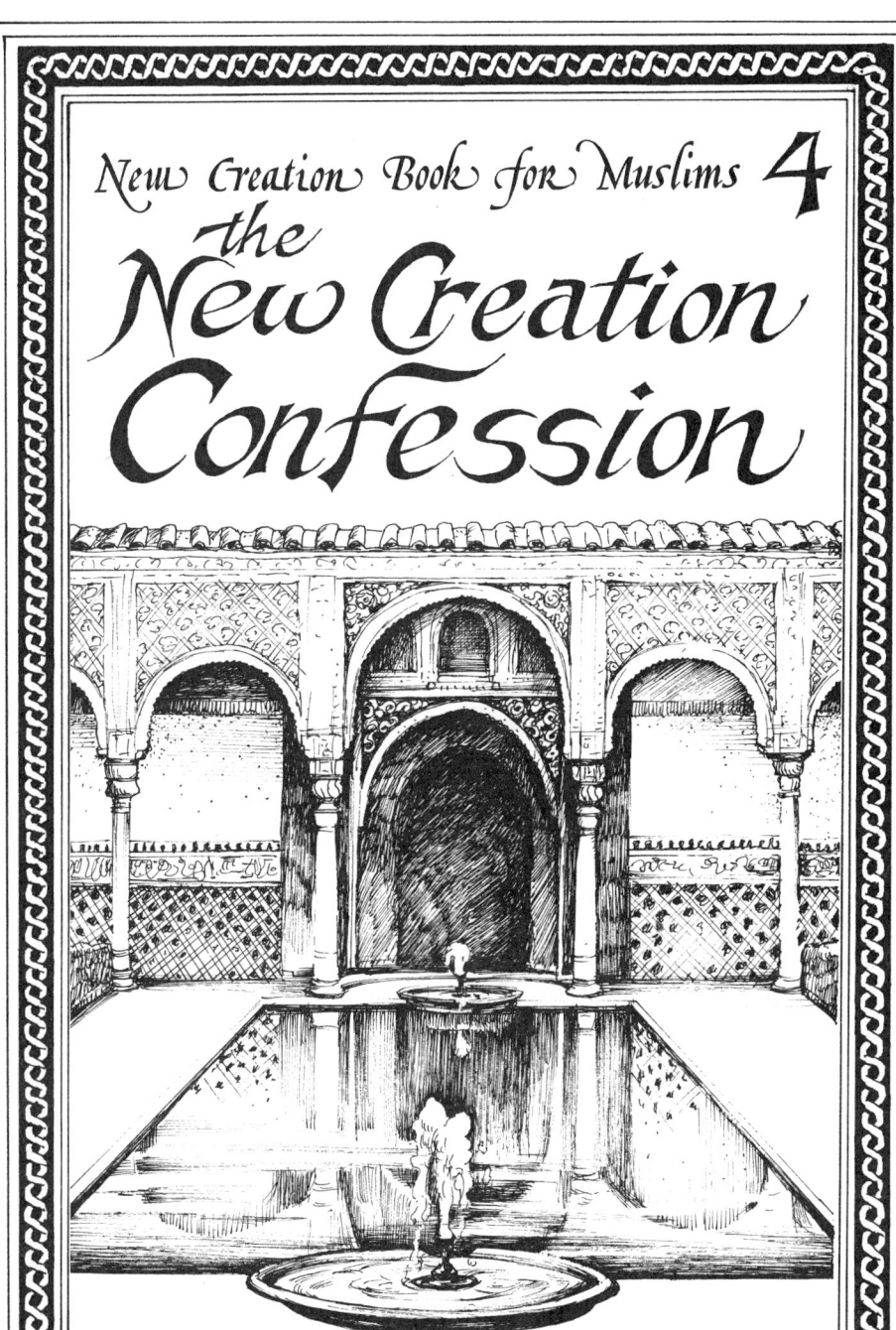

4

The New Creation Confession (Kalimah)

Did you know
that you must be made a new creation
by the personal Spirit of Allah?
Many people do not know this is true
but it is.
Isa who is the Truth says so.[1]
You must be spiritually formed and recreated
in the resurrection life he manifested
when Isa the Word of Allah
defeated death and rose from the grave.

This new creation that Isa insists on
is not something you can live without.
Nor can you avoid making a choice.
You yourself *will* choose
either by accepting, rejecting, or neglecting
the spiritual new birth
and thereby you will choose your eternal destiny.

There are *two* human races in the world:
one that has been born only once
and is moving toward
eternal divine separation and death;

---

[1] John 3:3

and the other that has been born twice
and is moving towards
eternal communion[1] and peace
and joy in the Eternal Spirit.
You must be born from the one race into the other.
You must be born again.

The human race was created to be perfect
and to reflect a perfect God.
But the whole family of man has broken God's laws
and has warped itself into a sinful disposition.[2]
Fulfilling the desires
of the old nature and of the old mind,
we are naturally culpable,
alienated and headed for judgment.
We need the new birth and the new life
of holy fellowship *(zamala)* in God's Risen Word Jesus (Isa)
in order than we may become spiritually alive.

The true path of life
is the path God has given us.
The Word of God (Isa)
did something in love on our behalf:
he mercifully took his own Death Judgment against us
upon himself.
Then he destroyed the power of death
by conquering the grave even as he died in our place.
Whoever says this is not true is lying
and is being seduced by a powerful delusion.
The wisdom of such a one
is not from above
but is earthly, sensual, devilish.[3]
But if you allow the truth
to touch your heart deeply,
and if you believe this truth in your heart

---

[1] This communion, known only by new creation Muslims, is called *wahda jamia al-muminin,* meaning "oneness of the fellowship of the believers."

[2] This is the *nafs al-ammarah,* the sin-prone soul, the rebellious spirit of man (Joseph 12:53 in the Qur'an).

[3] James 3:15

The New Creation Confession

and confess this truth with your lips,
you will begin the pilgrimage of true life.

What is next is thrilling and wonderful:
we confess this truth before the true believers
and we begin to digest and to enact this truth
with our body and our whole being,
and we follow this truth
and study this truth
with God's people forever.

Then what finally happens?
The Truth himself (*Isa)* takes us
from glory to glory.
Praise God! *Subhan Allah!*

HOW DOES ONE MAKE OUR *KALIMAH* OR CONFESSION?

But how does one become
a new creation Muslim
with Isa alive in one's life?
Only by faith in the Word of Allah.
Isa declared that the whole Book
spoke of nothing but his coming.[1]
And, true it is,
that Isa is the central theme of the true *Kitab*
and the focus of all our revelation of eternal life.
What other man *is* Allah's Word of eternal life?
Who but the death-conquering eternal Word in person
could say convincingly:
"I am the way, the truth, and the (eternal) life;
no man comes to Allah but through me"?[2]
Isa declared emphatically
that just as Allah has eternal life in himself,
so he has granted his Word to have eternal life in himself;[3]
for his Word is his heir
to whom Allah has given all authority

---

[1] Luke 24:34
[2] John 14:6
[3] John 5:26-27

and power and dominion to judge and to rule
the new age dawning in his light.

But only those in whom Isa is living
have new creation eyes and heart
with which to see and receive the truth of Isa,
truth inscribed in the written Word of God.
Either literally
or in prophetic foreshadowings
or symbols,
Isa and his truth are on every page
of the infallibly accurate *kitab* (Book).
Isa *is* the Word of God
and only his Words inspired by the Eternal Spirit
are the true words of Scripture.

If this is the truth,
why then does not everyone believe it?
Because the man without the Eternal Spirit of Allah
does not accept the words
that come from the Eternal Spirit of God,[1]
and no one can say that Isa
is the personal, eternal, divine Word
of God's Judgment
without the aid of the Eternal Spirit.[2]
No one can say that "there is no deity but God
and that Isa is the Word of God"
without the aid of the Eternal Spirit.
The natural man,
even if he is religious
or great by the measure of natural men,
has no taste for the saving Word Isa
spiritually discerned in the written Word of God.
This natural and unregenerated man
has received a different *kitab* (book)
and a different salvation message
and a different Jesus (Isa).[3]

---

[1] I Corinthians 2:14
[2] I Corinthians 12:3
[3] II Corinthians 11:4

The New Creation Confession

But the true *Kitab* plainly says
that if any man comes
bringing a different salvation message
let him be eternally condemned to hell.[1]
There are many imitations of Isa
that men in their cunning have preached.
But the only true Isa
is the one revealed in the infallible Word
once for all delivered to the people who belong to God.
No man can add to this revelation
and no man can take away from it.
It is imperishable and unchangeable.

Therefore, you must discern the true words of Isa.
And you must see Isa truly
in the true words of prophecy.
These immortal words
were given by revelation
through the personal Spirit of Allah
to those men of old who knew
personally the ever-living Word of God
even before the divine Word put on human form
as Isa al-Masih.[2]
In the prophets[3]
God had promised salvation
to all those who looked when they prayed
toward the direction[4]
where His Name would dwell.
The Name of God in Scripture

---

[1] Galatians 1:9
[2] I Peter 1:10-11
[3] II Chronicles 6:38
[4] The *qibla* is the direction in which acceptable prayer is to be offered. Isa said, "If you shall ask for anything in My name, I will do it." By this the Word of God was saying, that if you pray in *my direction*, your prayers will be answered. But, if you are an unbeliever in God's Word Isa, no matter in which direction you pray, "let not that man think that he shall receive anything of the Lord" (James 1:7). John 4:20-24 shows that since God is a Spirit, direction or place in themselves are not crucial. Knowing God is all-important. God cannot be known apart from His Word and Isa is His Word.

is his personal self-disclosure,
and God discloses himself by His Word.
God had promised that His Word
would meet with the people
and tabernacle among them
in the power of the Eternal Spirit.
Isa is that Word.
Isa is that Name.
Isa is that tent of meeting with God in the desert of this world,
Isa is that moveable pilgrim's feast,
that spiritual bread of display,
the one who came down from heaven
that all men might digest who he is
and live forever.
Isa is that mysterious lampstand
and that light of the niche (*mishkat-ul-anwar*)
that lights up the dead, dark hearts of men.
Isa is the Covenant Word of Eternal Life.
Isa is the pilgrim's acceptable sacrifice.

Sin led to the destruction
of the house of God in *al-Quds* (Jerusalem),
and to the continuing holocaust of our Exile.[1]
But if God did not spare the ancient children of Ibrahim,
he will not spare us either,
if we join them in their unbelief.[2]
And if judgment begins with the household of God
what shall be the fate of those
who disbelieve Isa's message?[3]
They too shall be judged
by the divine Word of Judgment
who is himself the indestructible House of Allah
willingly torn down by men, yes,
but only to mercifully make atonement (*takfeer*)
in order to be resurrected from the dead forever
by the Holy God of Ibrahim
as the true direction of our prayers.

---

[1] James 1:1; Romans 8:36.
[2] Romans 11:21
[3] I Peter 4:17

It is in *his* direction that we confess
through the enablement of Allah's Eternal Spirit,
"There is no deity but God,
and Isa is the Word of God."

OUR CONFESSION IN OUR ID UL-ADHA REMEMBRANCE

When we New Creation Muslims confess the saving truth
in our New Creation Id ul-Adha service,
our worship is more than mere lip service
or an empty religious ritual.
When we eat and drink in the Id ul-Adha of Isa,
we are renewing
Allah's solemn covenant promise to Ibrahim,[1]
his unchangeable contractual pledge
that constitutes the basis of our salvation.

THE ID UL-ADHA EXPLAINED

It says in the Qur'an
that if a pilgrim is prevented
from completing the *Hajj* (Pilgrimage),
"send an offering
for sacrifice."[2]
At the climax of the Hajj,
a sacrificial meal is eaten
that remembers the God (Allah)
who has been faithful to us
since the days of Ibrahim,
when Allah ransomed Ibrahim's heir
with a "momentous sacrifice."
Id ul-Adha is the "Feast of Sacrifice"
when pilgrims remember
Allah's act of divine mercy to Ibrahim.

---

[1] The nature of this covenant is important. In the Word of God it is not an agreement between equals as though we could save ourselves by keeping the covenant by our unaided will. We do not believe that we can save ourselves. Rather we believe that what God promised in His covenant to Ibrahim—our salvation with Ibrahim—He is bringing to pass.

[2] Cow. 2:196

All over the world,
a joyful feast of recollection is held
simultaneously at the time of the *hajj* (pilgrimage).
To remember Allah's mercy to Ibrahim
with a "more lively remembrance"
is the intention of the feast.
Not only in Mina (near Mecca),
but universally and corporately,
all the believers are to become pilgrims in spirit
by joining in the meal wherever they are.
Their purpose is to achieve not merely a remembrance
but a corporate identity
as a worshipping community (*ummah*).

The pilgrims who offer the sacrificial sheep
or other animal have read this saying:
"It is not their meat
nor their blood that reaches Allah."[1]

We read in the Kitab of the *Injil* (the New Testament)
that "it is not possible that the blood of bulls and goats
should take away sins,"[2]
and that it is only by being made just
by the sin-atoning blood of the Word of Allah Isa
that we can "be saved
from wrath through him."[3]
Whoever would prefer the blood of an animal
to the blood of the Word of Allah Himself
is no true submitter to Allah,
for "how much more shall the blood of il-Masih,
who through the eternal Spirit offered himself
without spot (he was sinless) to God,
purge your conscience
from dead works (self-righteousness religion)
to serve the living God?"[4]

---

[1]Pilgrimage 22:37
[2]Hebrews 10:4
[3]Romans 5:9
[4]Hebrews 9:14

COVENANT COMMUNION MEAL CELEBRATES VICTORY OVER SATAN

This occasion of Id ul-Adha is symbolically connected
to a perfect victory over Satan
by a stone-throwing ceremony
that points to the rejection of evil
in thought, word, and deed.
Do you remember when God
symbolized this same victory
by means of a stone-throwing shepherd boy?
Do you remember when God
got victory over Satan's warrior Goliath (*Jalut*)
through the boy warrior David (*Dawud*)?
It was through five stones,
and the first one thrown hit its mark.
David remembered how Allah had slain
another warrior, Pharoah (*Fir'aun*), at the Red Sea,
and David recalled how Allah then commanded
his people to make a *hajj* (pilgrimage)
from slavery to freedom and life.
Those Allah liberated from Pharaoh
were ordered to celebrate
Allah's victory standing up like pilgrims
eating in haste a sacrificial meal of remembrance.

It says in the Qur'an,
"In the past We granted
to Moses and Aaron
the Salvation and a Light
and a Remembrance (*dhikr*)."[1]
All over the world
Moses' sacrificial feast of pilgrimage
was celebrated at the same time of year,
whether the believers could make the Hajj
to the city of David or not.
It was a communion meal,
and was celebrated at the House of Allah in *al-Quds*

---

[1] The Prophets 21:48

and also in homes around the family table.
It was a communion meal,
because it emphasized the fellowship
with God and with the family
of true brothers in the faith.
The reason it was celebrated at the House of Allah
was to emphasize its significance for the covenant,
and the covenant-loyal God who was remembered
by those who partook of the meal.

At the time of the Hajj
on a special feast day,
the Id ul-Adha feast is celebrated today,
and those who do make the pilgrimage
celebrate it at the same time
as those who do not.
This universal communion
symbolizes the universal covenant loyalty of Allah.

HOW WE THROW A STONE AT *SHAITAN* (SATAN)

We who are new creation Muslims
join Da'ud in throwing a stone at Satan.
However, the stone we throw is a *spiritual* stone,
the Stone of Stumbling,
the Stone of the soon-coming Warrior Word Isa
whom David foreshadowed.

Those with new creation eyes can see this Stone
in the stone-sized piece of *khubis* (bread)
which we break off in remembrance
of the Word of Allah made flesh.
He is the Stone men stumble over to their eternal shame.
He is the Stone that Allah threw down to earth
to defeat the Devil
and to make atonement (*takfeer*) for our sins.
We who are new creation Muslims
join *Musa* (Moses) on his Hajj from slavery,
by partaking together of this sacrificial meal
that brings us into communion,

into the oneness of the fellowship of the believers:[1]
it is the Id ul-Adha Isawiya.

The *Injil* says that we are "strangers
and pilgrims on the earth."[2]
This means we are *in* the world
but we are not *of* the world,
for our power to live comes from the Eternal Spirit of Allah.
His inspired words tell us plainly
how we should oppose Satan:
"Dearly beloved, I beseech you as strangers and pilgrims,
abstain from fleshly lusts,
which war against the soul."[3]
We new creation Muslims do not simply partake of a sacrificial meal;
we submit our bodies as a living sacrifice.[4]

THE ID UL ADHA AND MUSA (*MOSES*)

"And remember we gave Moses the Scripture
and the Salvation."[5]
In the Taurat it says,
"And Moses wrote all the words of the Lord,
and rose up early in the morning,
and built an altar under the mountain,
and twelve pillars,
according to the twelve tribes of Israel.
And he sent young men of the children of Israel,
which offered burnt offerings,
and sacrificed peace offerings of oxen unto the Lord.
And Moses took half of the blood,
and put it in basins;
and half of the blood he sprinkled on the altar.

---

[1] *wahda jamia al-muminin*
[2] Hebrews 11:13
[3] I Peter 2:11
[4] Romans 12:1
[5] The Arabic word in this portion of the Qur'an is *furqan* or criterion, that is, between right and wrong. See Cow. 2:53

And he took the book of the covenant,
and read in the audience of the people:
and they said, 'All that the Lord hath said
will we do, and be obedient.'
And *Moses took the blood and sprinkled it on the people*,
and said, 'Behold *the blood of the covenant*
which the Lord hath made with you concerning all these words.'
Then went up Moses, and Aaron, Nadab, and Abihu,
and seventy of the elders of Israel:
And *they saw the God of Israel:*
and there was under His feet
as it were a pavement of sapphire stone,
as clear as heaven.
And upon the sheikhs of the children of Israel
He laid not his hand (in vengeance):
also they saw God (that is, they experienced the *sakinah*
and mystically beheld a vision of Allah)
and *they did eat and drink*." (Exodus 24:4-11)

The manipulation of the blood
in relation to the book of the covenant
was predictive of the Word who would take on flesh
and sacrificial blood as Isa al-Masih,
the Word of Allah.

DO YOU UNDERSTAND THAT THERE MUST BE A BLOOD APPEASEMENT OF GOD'S ANGER?

The blood Moses (*Musa*) sacrificed was also to appease God's anger.
Appeasement is crucial because of the right of God (*haqq Allah*)
in his righteous fury
to inflict on a culprit
the fearful penalty his sins deserve.
God is rightfully furious with the wicked everyday,
and the removal of this wrath by a rightfully acceptable gift
is the meaning behind the blood sacrifice of Moses.[1]

---

[1] see Romans 3:21ff., I John 2:2; Psalm 7:11; Numbers 14:18; Nahum 1:3

It was revealed to Moses
that God's furious penalty against the guilty culprit
is justly averted
only by sacrificing a victim
who stands in to take the place of the repentant sinner.
Allah mercifully allows this substitution
so that forgiveness will not be offered
in such a way as to make a mockery of justice.
Allah will allow no one's sins to go unpunished
without an acceptable sacrifice
to carry out the required sentence of justice
and to duly bear the pain of evil.
As long as the culprit knows he is guilty and culpable
and as long as he knows no justice has been exacted
by the punishment of an acceptable sacrificial victim,
then he has no peace with God because
he knows he cannot be purified for fellowship with Allah.
The angry wrath of Allah against injustice *must* be appeased,
and the justice of Allah must not be slighted.
A real victim must experience real death,[1]
and the real repentant contrition of faith
must lead the sinner
to stop committing such costly and death-dealing sins.
Only on this basis is there real forgiveness.
This alone is the basis for fellowship with Allah
including the privilege
of eating and drinking at his covenant table.

THE ID UL-ADHA AND ISA

Crucifixion is listed as one of the kinds
of punishment in the muslim law (*Sharia*).
In The Table Spread. 5:33,
we read that crucifixion indicates
"a heavy punishment in the Hereafter."
In the *Taurat*

---

[1] Woe to those who say that Isa did not die. Who is a bigger liar than the one who says that Jesus did not shed his blood to appease the wrath of God against sinners?

Moses says that "anyone who is hanged on a tree
is accursed by God."[1]
Hellish abandonment by God, then,
is what crucifixion signifies.

Isa the Word of Allah knew
that he had been commanded by Allah
to take away the sins of the world.
Isa knew that only he himself
as the perfect Word of Allah in flesh and blood
could fully experience the pain of the world's sin
and its hellish curse
and only he could acceptably take it away.
The written Word had commanded death for sins:
"it is the blood
that makes atonement for the soul;"[2]
and only the living Word, Allah's suffering Servant,
could take death away:
"God sent his Word and healed them...
the punishment that brought us peace was upon him,
and by his whip marks we are healed."[3]
Thus the living Word as our *Imam*
obeyed the written Word
and the unique destiny
there ordained for him.

Isa knew that there is hostility between Allah,
who is holy,
and sinful men who are not,
and that only the Word of Allah himself
could provide by his infinitely precious blood
the appeasement of the divine justice
and outrage against evil,
the appeasement that could honorably turn Allah
to a favorable attitude toward us.

---

[1] Deuteronomy 21:23
[2] Leviticus 17:11
[3] Psalm 107:20; Isaiah 53:5

The New Creation Confession

THE HOUSE MASJID OF ISA ON THE EVE OF THE FRIDAY OF ATONEMENT

On the night of Isa's betrayal and arrest
he met with his disciples in a room in al-Quds.
He had just given a washing (*wudu*)
to every one of his disciples' feet.
And they sat on the floor
with their shoes off.
There were no images in the room
and in that respect it looked very much like a mosque.

Isa himself seemed like an Imam speaking
to the key men of the mosque
or like a Sufi *Wali* (or *pir*) or religious leader with his *halaqah*.[1]

That night Isa would prove himself
to be the ultimately submitted One,
who said, "Not my will but thine be done."
Of what other man was it ever said
that he was the Word of Allah?
And who is more submitted to Allah
than his own Word?
Only a stutterer has speech unsubmitted to himself,
and no reverent person would imply that of Allah.
The name of the Word of Allah is Isa
and there is no other name given among men
whereby we must be saved.

No man who is not *the* Word of God
can place himself above Allah's unique and only Word.

His disciples sensed the God-inspired peace (the *sakinah*)
as they looked into his dark piercing eyes.
That Isa was the Word of Allah incognito
was not unveiled to Judas,
who in his blind rebellion
mistook Isa for an ordinary mortal.

---

[1] A *halaqah* is a "circle" of students or disciples of a given teacher or "master."

But this aura was sensed
by the Apostle *Yahya* (John) and the rest.

Many today are blind like Judas.
And even many so-called believers
are too blind to discern the Word of Judgment incognito
in the broken bread and the outpoured cup
of the Id ul-Adha of Isa.
These hypocrites eat and drink judgment upon themselves
because they refuse to repent of their sins
and submit to the Judge who took our judgment
signified by the broken bread and the uplifted cup.

THE ID UL-ADHA AND *TALUT* (SAUL) KNOWN AS THE APOSTLE PAUL

We read of a pilgrimage
performed by one of the disciples of Isa.
His name was *Talut* or Saul
because he had been named after King Saul
and was from the same tribe.
Saul was a great Jewish mullah,
a great learned man so zealous in his religious knowledge
that he persecuted all those who said that they
were submitting to Allah through Isa.
However, on the road to Damascus in Syria
this mullah from Turkey was struck blind
by the risen Word of Allah Himself, Isa the Messiah.
It was then that Saul began a series of religious pilgrimages
that each led him inevitably back to al-Quds
as he travelled the world as the Apostle Paul.
To show that the Good News is not based on
religious knowledge
or on the burdens of ritual or men's good deeds
but on the grace of God through Isa His Word alone,
God raised this man Saul up
and prospered his ministry the most.
He had been a persecutor of the righteous.
He did not deserve to be saved.
He deserved to die.
He did not deserve a mullah's honorific position.
He deserved no place of honor in the Lord's house.

The New Creation Confession

Yet God exalted his ministry the most
because God is gracious and kind
and there is no place in his house
for the mentality of the proud Pharisee
who thinks he can put God into his debt
by his religious profession or his own righteousness.

Saul, also named Paul,
made the greatest pilgrimage of all the apostles.
Paul journeyed from Europe to *al-Quds*
carrying alms (*zakat*) and/or *sadaqa* (free will offerings)
as an act of loving identification.
Paul was willing to participate
in the rituals of his former faith
in order to prove,
even if the proof cost him his life,
that he was a true-to-his-traditions submitter to Allah.
Why was this proof so important to Paul?
Because he knew that traditions were not the issue
—what mattered was becoming a new creation.
Paul was willing to become like the sons of Ishmael
to win the sons of Ishmael
and he was willing to become like the sons of Israel
to win the sons of Israel.
Paul was willing to make any sacrifice
—even seal his inerrant testimony with martyrdom—
if it would bring the Word of Salvation Isa
to the lost peoples of the world
and lead them to the straight path.

Paul was a prophet
and he could see with the eyes of the Eternal Spirit
that a military holocaust was coming
and that the False Messiah (*al-Dajjal*)
would deceive and destroy many
whose ears would be tickled by a false Gospel.
Therefore, Paul led people everywhere
to repent and take a death *ghusl* (Romans 6)
and pray and give alms
and celebrate the Id ul-Adha Isawiya
"with those who call on the Lord with a pure conscience."
For Paul had read in the prophet Isaiah (61:6)

how believers as "ministers of our God"
would see the riches of a harvest of souls
flow from the Nations to the faithful pilgrims of Allah.

THE ID UL-ADHA AND IBRAHIM

"By faith Ibrahim,
when he was called
to go out into a place
which he should after receive
for an inheritance,
obeyed;
and he went out,
not knowing whither he went."[1]

And when Ibrahim was tested,
he offered up his only heir,
just as Allah's only heir,
His everlasting Word
(who will inherit and judge the world)
was offered up by Allah.
But when was Isa tested?
When did this happen?
When Isa the Word of Allah
learned obedience through what he suffered
as Ibrahim's Lamb of God
who offered himself to make us heirs with him
of the Kingdom of Allah
by faith.

Ibrahim loved not the world,
neither the things that are in the world,[2]
but he looked for a city
whose builder and maker was God,
and he rejoiced to see the day
of Isa al-Masih

---

[1] Hebrews 11:8
[2] I John 2:15

who was the *qibla* (the direction of prayer)
toward which Ibrahim's hope was directed.[1]

Did you not know that Allah is our exalted Father?
This is why he chose a man
whose name was Exalted Father (Abram)
with whom to make his eternal covenant.
Then God gave him a new name, Ibrahim (Father of Nations),
promising him that is what he would become.[2]

In chapter 17 of the first book of the *Taurat*
God promised Ibrahim
that He would save those who shared his faith.
God made a contract with Ibrahim to that effect,
making the sign and seal of the contract circumcision,
which was itself a sign of the circumcision of the inner man,
the purification (*tahara*) of the heart and the spirit
which is regeneration, the new birth.

In Genesis 18:2, when God
makes a visit to Ibrahim,
Ibrahim hurries to get water.
Isa used water as Ibrahim did,
prior to a similar meal of communion with God.[3]

Isa led his disciples in ceremonially washing their hands
before the communion meal of the covenant of Ibrahim,
and then he washed their feet afterward (John 13:5).
Thus they remembered the covenant God sealed with his people
at the Red Sea of Salvation
and at the *sibghat Allah* total ablution
when each disciple went under the water
and was raised to newness of life in Allah.

Notice, then, that admission
to the communion meal of the Covenant of Ibrahim
involves a prior water ceremony,

---

[1] see Hebrews 11:10; John 8:56
[2] Genesis. 17:5-8
[3] Genesis 18:4-8

which is itself an outward sign
of the inward purging of sin through faith and the grace of God.

In calling all people to prepare for the Coming One,
the Lamb of God who takes away the sins of the world,
Yahya (John the Baptist) demanded a total ablution
formerly taken only by the unclean (a *ghusl* bath)
because Yahya, like all the other true prophets before him,
insisted that all men
were unclean at heart before God.
No one is good but God
and His Word who was God from the beginning,
for in the beginning was the Word
and the Word was with God
and the Word was God.
Then the Word came on the scene as a good man Isa.
If any other man says that he has not sinned
he is a liar
and the good Word of God (Isa)
is not in him.[1]

When *Yahya* (John the Baptist) perceived
that the Messiah was sinless,
Yahya hesitated to bathe Isa in a *ghusl* bath.
But realizing the priestly character of his office as Masih,
and that the law of Moses
required the priests to bathe
before they began their ministry,[2]
Isa submitted to the *ghusl*
in order to fulfill all righteousness,
including a righteous example.

(If the Messiah himself took this water rite,
and commanded all of his true followers to submit to him in it,
what monumental ignorance or unfounded fear or pride is there
in any man or woman in the world
that he or she should refuse to do likewise?)

---

[1] I John 1:10
[2] Lev.16:4 etc

The New Creation Confession

Ibrahim was given to us for our admonition (I Cor. 10:11).
Ibrahim obeyed God
with water and a communion meal in Genesis 18.
We should study this account and imitate Ibrahim:
"And the Lord appeared to Ibrahim
in the plains of Mamre:
and he sat in the tent door
in the heat of the day.
And he lifted up his eyes and looked,
and, lo, three men stood by him:
and when he saw them,
he ran to meet them from the tent door,
and bowed himself toward the ground,
and said,
'My Lord, if now I have found favor in thy sight,
pass not away, I pray thee,
from thy servant.
Let a little water be fetched,
and wash your feet,
and rest yourselves under the tree:
and I will fetch a morsel of bread,
so you can be refreshed;
after that you shall pass on:
now that you have come to your servant.'
And they said, 'Very well, do as you say.'"[1]

In verse 13, when the three are with Ibrahim,
the text says it is the Lord addressing Ibrahim.
In verse 8, when they eat, Ibrahim is experiencing
a communion meal with God.
At another crucial time,
Ibrahim experienced the saving presence of God.
In Genesis 22:9 it says,
"And they came to the place
which God had told him of;
and Ibrahim built an altar there."

The altar was an altar of sacrifice.
It says in Genesis 22:6

---

[1]Genesis 18:1-5

that the son of Ibrahim
carried the wood for the sacrifice,
just as later Isa the son of Ibrahim
would carry the wood (*khashabah*) for the sacrifice.
Ibraham was going to show his love for God
by giving his only heir,
just as it says in another place
that God so loved the world
that he gave his only heir,
his everlasting Word Isa,
in order that whosoever
believes in him
should not perish
but have everlasting life.[1]

The story continues:
"And Ibrahim stretched forth his hand,
and took the knife to slay his son.
And the angel of the Lord
called unto him out of heaven,
and said,
'Ibrahim, Ibrahim.'
And he said,
'Here am I.'
And he said,
'Lay not your hand upon the lad,
neither do any thing unto him;
for now I know that you fear God,
seeing you have not withheld your son,
your only son from me.'
And Ibrahim lifted up his eyes,
and looked,
and behold behind him
a ram caught in a thicket by his horns;
and Ibrahim went and took the ram,
and offered him up for a burnt offering
in the stead of his son."[2]

---

[1] John 3:16
[2] Genesis 22:10-13

The New Creation Confession

The new creation Id ul-Adha that new creation Muslims
celebrate is also a test of faith,
and we are to examine ourselves to be sure
that we are in the faith,
before we partake.

As we partake, we remember that God
provided a sacrifice for Ibrahim
and the sacrifice died
so that Ibrahim's heir and promised inheritance
might be raised to new life and live forever.
We praise Allah that we are heirs of Ibrahim
because we share the fulfillment of what was promised him.
The Messiah Isa came as the Lamb of God
and provided an eternal sacrifice for Ibrahim
and all the heirs of his faith,
so that as Ibrahim's sons
we too may be raised to new life and live forever!

THE ID UL-ADHA OF ISA SERVICE INTRODUCTION

We know perfectly well
that supposedly merit-earning religious observances
will not save us.
We remember that all but two
of those who followed Musa out of Egypt
died in the wilderness
without entering *al-Muqaddasa* (the Holy Land).
They too kept their religious practices,
but without a new nature even they could not please Allah,
and their rotting bodies littered the desert.
They had bread from heaven
and they had water from the rock,
just as we have bread and water,
but these alone could not save them
and neither can these religious symbols save us.

They passed through the Sea
and so they all received a death *ghusl* initiation
into the *ummah* of Musa in cloud and sea.
This water prefigured the death *ghusl*
through which you are now also delivered to safety.

This *wudu* of Isa is not the washing away of bodily uncleanness
but rather it is the obedient appeal to God of a clear conscience.

And it brings deliverance from the guilt and the penalty
and the power and the presence of sin
through the resurrection of Isa the Word of Allah,
who died and was buried for us
so that our sins could be paid for.
He rose from the dead for us so that we might be forgiven
and raised with Him to be recreated in His likeness.
And yet, though the *ummah* of Musa had the death *ghusl*
and the bread and the water of the Rock of the Kingdom,
Isa the eternal Word of Allah,
nevertheless, because of their rancorous unbelief
they nearly all perished in the desert
and did not enter into the promised rest.
These events happened as symbols to warn us
not to try to counterbalance with merit-earning good works
the evil things we might otherwise fatally set our hearts on.

Therefore, we are to take no part
in the *Id ul-Adha Isawiya* (the Sacrifice Feast of Isa)
without applying moral scrutiny
to our lives and behavior.

(The following service is best conducted
while seated on the floor, shoes off,
with the messianic Imam
leading the prayers and prostrations.)

THE SERVICE BEGINS WITH THE IMAM TAKING THE *KHUBIS*
AND THE GRAPE JUICE AND SPEAKING

It follows that anyone who eats the bread
and drinks the cup of the Lord unworthily
will be guilty of desecrating the body and the blood
of the Id ul-Adha Lamb who is the atoning Word of Allah,
Isa al-Masih.
We must discern His broken body in the bread
and His covenant-sealing blood in the cup.
We must remember that the Word who reigns
in our hearts as Lord

The New Creation Confession

died as the Lamb
for our sins,
lest we forget and continually indulge our sins.
Each believer must examine himself
before eating his share of the bread
and drinking from the cup.
For he who eats and drinks
eats and drinks judgment on himself
if he does not discern the Body that was broken for our sins.

(Those who have obeyed Isa the Word of Allah
by submitting to the *sibghat* Allah
may follow the prostrations of the messianic Imam.)

The ceremonial means of initiating the New Covenant
would normally be the *sibghat Allah*.
This is commanded of all believers
at the time they formally commit their lives to obey
Isa the Word of Allah.
He is obeyed as the One to reign in their hearts
as *Mawla* (Lord) and *Wahid Allah* (The Unique One from God)
and *Nasr Allah* (Savior).

> (The Messianic Imam reads:)
> Let us now have a few moments of silence
> as we prostrate to Allah
> and remember the day of our *sibghat Allah,*
> how we were buried in the water with him
> and experienced a total immersion *ghusl*
> as a funeral ritual bath,
> or we remember how we experienced a once-for-all *wudu*
> preparing us for a new life of prayer.
> It was not the water that was important
> so much as what it signified:
> that our bodies are dead to sin
> and that on that day we ceremonially entered into
> a sharing in Isa's death, praise be unto Him.
> In the silence about to commence
> each believer shall allow the Eternal Spirit of Allah
> to conduct a *tahara* through our flesh
> and purge out in confession all the sin
> in order that we may be pronounced 'clean' by our Lord.

(Read the following together after a few moments' silence):

"The next day", the Book of Allah says,
"*Yahya* saw Isa coming toward him and said,
"Look! There is the Lamb of Allah.
It is he who takes away the sin of the world.'"

MAWLA, WE CONFESS OUR SINS
If we confess our sins,
he is just,
and may be trusted
to forgive our sins
and cleanse us from every kind of wrong.

(Messianic Imam reading:)
Your sins are forgiven you for His name's sake.

(All the people reading:)
As Musa sprinkled the blood on the people
to seal that covenant,
so we are sprinkled with the blood of Isa
to seal the New Covenant.
We are united in this *Id ul-Adha* meal of the covenant
as the *ummah* of the Lamb of Allah
who takes away the sins of the world.
We belong to one another forever
and to the Lord.
By the way we love each other
may we discern that we are the Lord's Body
bought back from the dead at great price.

(Messianic Imam reading:)
Form your own judgment on what I say.
When we bless the cup of blessing,
is it not a means of sharing
in the atoning blood of Isa al-Masih?
When we break the bread,
is it not a means of sharing in the body
and the ummah of Isa al-Masih?
Because there is one loaf, we,

The New Creation Confession

many as we are, are one body.
For it is one loaf of which we all partake.
There is indeed nothing eternal but a new creation,
and we are all one ummah,
the spiritual people of Ibrahim,
submitters to Allah through His eternal Word, Isa al-Masih.
(Holding up the bread)
For the Passover tradition (appropriate for *Id ul-Adha*)
which I handed on to you
came to me from the Lord Himself:
that the Lord on the night of His arrest,
took bread and, after giving thanks to God,
broke it and said:
'This is my body, which is for you; do this
as a memorial of me.' (Reader breaks bread.)

(The Reader holds up the Cup)
In the same way, he took the cup after supper
at the end of his pilgrimage
to where He would make His departure at al-Quds.
Realizing Himself to be the Eternal Life of Allah
offered as the *Id ul-Adha* of Allah to the world,
he said: "This is the New Covenant
sealed by my blood.
Whenever you drink it, do this
as a memorial of me."

(Reader pours out from the pitcher into the cup.)
"For every time you eat this bread and drink this cup,
you proclaim the death of the Lord until He comes."

(The bread and the cups are distributed from person to person until all have partaken together.)

(The Reader:) Let us partake and worship the Lord. Maranatha.
(All prostrate and raise their hands with praise saying
"*Subhan Allah*—Glory to God! *Subhanaka*—Praise to Thee!
Al-Hamdu li-lah—the praise is God's! *Allahu Akbar*—God is Greater!")

(The Reader:) Let me urge any of you
who have not yet submitted to Allah

in the *sibghat Allah* to do so in order that
you will not exclude yourself
from celebrating the Id ul-Adha Isawiya with us
at our next opportunity,
should the Second Coming
of the Word of Allah delay.

SCRIPTURES FOR POSSIBLE ADDITIONAL HEALING SERVICE

If you will diligently listen to the voice of the Lord your God,
    and will do that which is right in is sight,
    and will give attention to his coommandments,
    and keep all his sacred laws,
I will put none of these diseases upon you
which I have brought upon the people of Egypt[1],
for I am the Lord who heals you.
Is anyone sick among you?
Let him call for the *sheikhs* (elders)
of the *jami'* (congregation)
and let them pray over him
anointing him with oil in the name of the Lord.
And the prayer of faith will make the sick person well, and the Lord wil raise him up.
And if he has committed sins, he will be forgiven.[2]
Satan would send accusers to say that it is for our sin that Allah uses sickness to bring us into condemnation.[3]
But there is now no condemnation
or those who are in (the new life of) Isa al-Masih.[4]
When he made the "momentous sacrifice"[5] for us
he was wounded and bruised (to atone) for
our rebellion and perverseness.
He took the beating and lashing (we deserved)
in order that we might have peace (with God)

---

[1]Exodus 15:26
[2]James 5:14-15
[3]Job. 11:6 *JB*
[4]Romans 8:1
[5]Those Ranged in Ranks 37:107

The New Creation Confession 125

and with His stripes we *were* healed
(of sin's condemnation and the second death,
which is separation from God).[1]
Therefore, as Isa himself said,
Your faith has made you whole[2].
Receive your healing[3].

---

[1] Isaiah 53:5
[2] Matthew 9:22
[3] Luke 18:42. Although we all believe that God can heal, and in many cases will heal as we trust in Him, we certainly have to allow for the fact that at times He may allow a healing not to occur for reasons tha simple mortals may not fully understand. (Death is a part of the human condition, which means that human beings generally have at least one illness that is not healed!) Unless we at least note this, inquirers may lose faith if they are not healed every time they pray.

New Creation Book for Muslims 5

The Pilgrimage for New Creation Muslims

5

The New Creation Pilgrimage

The New Creation 'Id ul-Adha
is the feast of sacrifice of Ibrahim[1]
who remembered with a solemn sacrifice
when Allah spared his heir.
This celebration looked forward to Ibrahim's greatest heir,
the Messiah Isa, who is the Messenger of Allah
and his Word[2]
the one who will inherit and judge the whole world.
As such, Isa is the Messenger of Ibrahim's covenant *('ahd)*.
The Messianic 'Id al-Adha commemorates
Isa's momentous sacrifice or *beezah 'azim*[3]
at the end of his pilgrimage
in the holy land of Ibrahim (*Muqaddasa*),
when Allah spared all his heirs
by providing the eternal Lamb of God
who takes away the sin of the world.

---

[1] Some may object to the use of 'Id ul-Adha as a name for a contextualized communion since *'Id ul-Adha* refers to a specific day of the year, whereas communion is celebrated more frequently. However, the Lord's Seder is a once-a-year festival (Passover) that Isa turned into a remembrance meal of more frequent celebration. Since both Passover and *'Id ul-Adha* have connections with Abraham's sacrifice and with the concept of mystical communion in a world-embracing *ummah* or community, the choice of contextualized terminology seems apt.
[2] The Women.4:171;Malachi 3:1;John 1:1
[3] Those Ranged in Ranks.37:107

THE ETERNAL WORD OF ALLAH

The Word of Allah always existed
as the Servant (*abd*) of Allah.
Before the Word took human form as Isa the Messiah
he was still personally existent,
and reflected the likeness of Allah
as the heavenly Word of Judgment
whose personal name was Son of Man.[1]
He is the pre-existent Word of Allah,
his uncreated and co-eternal agent
in creation and redemption and judgment.
More than the living heavenly pattern
around whom the Eternal Spirit
inspired the true *Kitab* (Book) of *Taurat* and *Injil*,
Isa is also both the death-conquering Messenger of the covenant
and the life-giving Message of the covenant.[2]

He is, in fact, the covenant.
The Dead Sea Scrolls incorruptibly preserve
the prediction of the prophet Isaiah who,
seven hundred years before Isa the man arrived,
spoke of him as the covenant:
"Behold my Servant, whom I uphold;
my chosen one in whom I myself delight.
I have put my Spirit upon him:
He shall bring forth judgment to the Nations
...the islands shall wait for his law (or teaching)
...I the Lord have called thee (the Servant of Allah)
in righteousness
and will hold thine hand,
and *will keep thee for a covenant* of the people,
for a light to the Gentiles."[3]
You have heard of the saying,
"We have already, beforehand,
taken the covenant (*'ahida*) of Adam,

---

[1] Daniel 7:13-17; John 1:1,51
[2] Romans 1:9
[3] Isaiah 42:1,4, 6

The New Creation Pilgrimage

but he forgot: and we found
on his part *no firm resolve*." [1]
Only the indwelling Word who is the covenant
can put his own eternal "firm resolve" in us,
for he is the promised indwelling law
to be written indelibly on the heart.[2]
As the prophet Malachi says,
the Messiah would be called,
"The Messenger of the Covenant" and the "Lord"[3]
You have heard this saying:
"When Jesus came
with clear signs, he said:
'...Fear Allah and obey me.'"[4]
The "clear signs" Jesus came with
were the miracles he used to attest the eternal covenant
he would institute as the Lamb of God.
On that night, the night of the climax of his pilgrimage,
he took the bread and the cup
and he said that these were now the memorials
for remembrance of his body and his blood
of the New and Eternal Covenant of Allah.

"Remember we took
a Covenant (*mithaq*) from the Children
of Israel..." [5]

This covenant was celebrated each year
in the Passover meal,
where remembrance was made of how Allah
saved them at the Red Sea
and gave them the law on Mount Sinai.
It was at such a feast (*id*) of pilgrimage (*hajj*)
that Isa instituted a meal of remembrance
in which he would be the Lamb of God,

---

[1] Ta Ha. 20:115
[2] Jeremiah 31:33
[3] Malachi 3:1; see also Jeremiah 23:6
[4] Gold Adornments. 43:63
[5] Cow. 2:83

and his blood would effect a new exodus from sin,
a new *hijrah* (emigration) from sin and death
for all true new creation submitters to Allah.

Those who deny this truth have these two sayings
of their own to refute them:
"*Isa al-Masih* (Jesus the Messiah)
was the Messenger of Allah and his Word."[1]
"And they (the children of Israel) said:
'Allah took our promise not to believe
in a Messenger unless He showed us a sacrifice'"[2]

The common people did believe in great numbers
in the sacrifice that Isa showed them,
but the proud and self-comfortable religious leaders
did not believe and they led the people away from the truth.

So it is today.

Isa himself said,
"If the blind lead the blind,
both will fall into a pit."

But we who are *Khalq Jadeed* (New Creation) Muslims
do in fact submit to Allah
by obeying him,
by embarking on a pilgrimage of witness
through the New Creation *Wudu* of Allah
to the New Creation *'Id ul-'Adha*.

Just as Musa passed through death
at the Red Sea,
so we pass through the death of our old life
at the death ghusl of Allah.
Just as the dead body of a Muslim
receives a total ablution (*ghusl*),
so by faith we put to death our body of sinful disposition
when we take the *ghusl* of *sibghat Allah* (baptism).

---

[1]Women. 4:171
[2]The House of Imran. 3:183

The New Creation Pilgrimage

Just as those with Musa
ate a sacrificial meal
to remember their *sibghat Allah* at the Red Sea,
so we who are messianic Muslims
eat a sacrificial meal
to remember our *sibghat Allah* at the command of Isa.

You must know that a *ghusl* (total ablution)
was necessary for a dead body being buried,
and that it was also in order
before the *'Id* prayers.

As with Moses and the Passover Seder Table,
so with Isa and the Lord's Table
—no one could be admitted to the Table where the covenant was remembered
unless the covenant had been properly initiated.
Isa commanded that the sign of covenant initiation
be the death *ghusl* of Allah,
the *wudu* of Allah.

Do you understand that you would normally
submit to *sibghat Allah* before taking
the New Creation *'Id ul-'Adha* with the other believers?

This water probe is designed by God
to be an overt sign of your submission to his authority.

God has commanded us in his infallibly accurate Word
not only to confess Isa
as Allah's Word of authority
and our Lord
in our private and congregational prayers;
God has also commanded us to confess him
in the *sibghat Allah* and the *'Id ul-Adha* Isawiya.
Now the question is,
will you submit to Allah and truly obey Isa from your heart?

A baptism was in order before the Passover supper
and before the Last Supper of Isa
when he finished his pilgrimage
and offered himself as the eternal *'Id ul-Ahda,*

the Feast of Sacrifice,
the Lamb of God,
the bread of life that comes down from heaven.
Isa spoke of mystically ingesting
the everlasting benefits of his sacrifice in this way:
"Whoso eateth my flesh,
and drinketh my blood,
hath eternal life;
and I will raise him up on the last day."[1]
We also remember that Isa said of himself,
Even the Messiah "came not to be served,
but to serve,
and to give his life as a ransom for many."[2]
In the Dead Sea Scrolls the prophet (Isaiah)
said the Messiah would "bear the sin of many."
Isa was fulfilling that prophecy
made 700 years before,
and the *dhabh* (sacrifice) fulfillment
was the key to the self-awareness
of his whole life's purpose.

We who are *Khalq Jadeed* (New Creation) Muslims
do not have to make a sacrifice
in the Valley of Mina in the vicinity of Mecca,
because the object of our pilgrimage[3]
has already made the perfect sacrifice for us.

Pilgrims are eager in Mecca to touch or kiss the Black Stone
as if it represents the right hand of God,
with whom they are renewing their covenant.
But we who are Khalq Jadeed Muslims believe this verse:
"Kiss the Son[4]

---

[1] John 6:54
[2] Mark 10:45
[3] Philippians 3:14
[4] The term *ibnullah* defines Isa as Allah's Grand Khalifa for the world, the inheritor of all that Allah has planned. So, too, as we enter into his service of surrender or "islam" to Allah, we also become new creation "sons of Allah"—that is, we become heirs to inherit and rule over Allah's world. Isa modelled our sonship by his perfect surrender as the "Lamb of God," the

The New Creation Pilgrimage

lest he be angry
and ye perish from the way."[1]
He is the chief cornerstone[2]
of the House of Allah,
(a temple not made with hands)
and Ibrahim rejoiced to see his day,[3]
for He is the right hand of God's righteousness[4]
and in him alone is the covenant renewed.[5]

When we stand up at the New Creation *Id ul-Adha*
it is not because the pilgrims stand
to perform the *wuquf* (the "standing")
from noon until sunset at 'Arafat.
We stand because whoever eats this bread and drinks this cup
preaches the death of the Lord until he comes.[6]
Therefore, we confess Isa in prayer,
we confess him before true believers,
we confess him in the *sibghat Allah,*
and we confess him in the *Id ul-Adha.*
The Scripture says,
"If you confess with your lips the Lord Isa (Jesus)
and believe in your heart that God raised him from the dead
(he died for our sins and was buried
and rose again on the third day
according to the Scriptures),
you shall be saved."[7]

When those pilgrims stand under the scorching sun
on the ninth day of the final *hajj* month,

---

momentous sacrifice—Qur'an 37:107, the *Qurbani* for the sins of the world by which man enters the very nearness—*Qurbi*—of Allah wherein dwells His Power and Glory.

[1] Psalm 2:12
[2] Ephesians 2:20
[3] John 8:56
[4] Isaiah 41:10
[5] Jer. 31:33; Mt.26:28
[6] I Cor. ll::6
[7] Romans 10:9; I Corinthians 15:3-4; Isaiah 53; Daniel 9:26; Hosea 6:2

they pray and recite verses of the Quran,
hoping that their sins will be forgiven.

But we know our sins
are already forgiven in Isa's name,
and a day is coming when all those who reject Isa
will stand before the scorching heat of the Word of God.

When we take Isa's cup,
then we also remember that Isa said,
"Whoever is thirsty,
let him come to me and drink.
...whoever drinks of the water
that I shall give him
shall never thirst;
but the water that I shall give him
shall be in him a well of water
springing up into everlasting life."[1]
The *Kaaba* has a door,
and the shrine itself
is called the House of Allah.
But Isa said, "I am the door,"
and we know that no one enters
the Spiritual House of Allah
but by Him.

Isa the Word of Allah
who is the likeness of His glory
is the object of our pilgrimage.
"We all, with open face,
beholding as in a glass
the glory of the Lord,
are changed into the same image
from glory to glory,
even as by the Spirit of the Lord."[2]
"Beloved, now are we the sons of God
(not in a progenitive sense, but in the sense that we
have been "fathered" by the new birth

---

[1] John 7:37; 4:14
[2] II Cor. 3:18

The New Creation Pilgrimage

to now have the likeness of God
writing Himself into our hearts)
and it does not yet appear what we shall be;
but we know that,
when he shall appear,
we shall be like him;
for we shall see him as he is."[1]
So we forget what lies behind
and press on to the object of our pilgrimage, Isa al-Masih,
whose world-wide body of true believers
is the true House of Allah,
whose house we are[2].
We pray that many would have their eyes opened
to see the Kingdom of Allah,
to see his world-wide house,
the universal body of true believers
seated spiritually already with Him in heavenly places
where his true house stands indestructible.

O Lord!
Grant this house (the house of Isa the Word of Allah)
greater honor, veneration, and awe;
and grant those who venerate it
and make (spiritual) pilgrimage to it
peace and forgiveness.
O Lord! Thou art the peace.
Peace is from Thee.
So we know that we have passed from death to life
and that you will greet us (on the day of Judgment)
with the same greeting you gave the disciples
on Resurrection morning:
"*As Salama Alaikum*," or "Peace be unto you."[3]

WHAT THE *SIBGHAT ALLAH* IS AND IS NOT

"O ye who believe!
Approach not prayers

---

[1] I John 3:2
[2] I Cor. 3:9
[3] John 20:19

with a mind befogged,
until you can understand
all that ye say,
nor in a state of ceremonial impurity
(except when travelling on the road),
until after washing your whole body."[1]

"O ye who believe!
when ye prepare
for prayer, wash..."[2]
"...And He (Allah) is the All-Hearing,
the All-Knowing,
the baptism of God: (*sibghat Allah*)
And who can baptize better than Allah?
And it is He whom we worship."[3]
The ceremony of *sibghat Allah*
does not represent conversion from religious affiliation.
The Jews who were baptized were not using the ceremony
to indicate that they had changed their religion
from their old religion to a new one.
The ceremony was first used to indicate
a renewal movement within the one religion
of those submitting to God.
The ceremony of *sibghat Allah*
represents a conversion from sin,
not from one religion to another.
It is a rite of passage from the old life to the new life,
not from the old religion to the new religion.
New creation Muslims are still *Muslims* (submitters to God).[4]

---

[1] The Women. 4:43
[2] The Table Spread. 5:6
[3] Cow.2:137-138
[4] Paul seldom allowed the false teachers to monopolize words their hearers considered attractive labels. Take for instance the word "circumcision," which certain legalists dangled before Paul's disciples. Notice that in Philippians 3:3 Paul does not allow this attractive word to be captured by them, but snatches it back, disinfects it of any content from their false teaching, pours pure Biblical content into the world, and then commandeers the word into the service of the Great Commission of Matthew 28:19-20. Those believers in Isa who needlessly forfeit the use of the word "Allah" or

They are more fully in submission ("*islam*") to Him.[1]

If certain religionists want to use a water ritual as a rite of passage from one religion to another, then let them go ahead and do it. But let no one confuse what they are doing (having people radically change their religious labels and their Muslim names on their identity card, expecting people to alienate themselves from their culture, etc.) with what we are doing.

The *Sibghat Allah* is not the cleansing of the body,
nor does the water magically remove the demonic
or cleanse sin (I Peter 3:21).

This is a humanly contrived teaching which ignorant men
have tried to add to God's Word.
In this misunderstanding, Muslim religionists can be as guilty
as Christian religionists.
For example, nowhere does the Qur'an teach that the *wudu*
(washing prior to the five-times-daily prayers)
cleanses from sin.
Some believe that when a believer
washes his face, hands and feet,
every sin connected with these parts of the body
will come out as a result of ablution.
But we know that only the infinitely precious blood
of the Masih's sacrifice can wash away sins,
and our faith is in his blood alone.

The fallacy of believing in the cleansing power of mere water
is obvious enough:
if we really believe the water cleanses and makes holy,
why do we not use water to make swine's flesh
ritually pure and usable?
Those who have concocted these sorts of beliefs
are trapped by their own fallacies.

---

the word "Muslim" may do so, but they may not claim that by doing so they are following Pauline methodology.

[1] Some may object that we are using these terms apart from their legitimate use. However, the Injil expresses this: `Submit therefore to God'—James 4:7

However, we recommend that new believers walk softly
and do not criticize Islam
or the Biblical interpretations of fellow believers,[1]
or their families' beliefs or practices.
Realizing you are a new believer,
you may not yet know fully
what has happened to you.
Therefore you be very careful and prayerful
about how you share your faith and with whom.
It might be best to consult your fellowship leader
before you take such a serious
and potentially dangerous step.

Possessing the gift of a changed nature, a new creation,
not changing one's government loyalty or religious label,
is all that can save anyone on the day of God's judgment.
There is only one eternally efficacious Biblical baptism
and this is the deep immersion into the new creation waters,
the primal waters,
the in-the-beginning waters
of the hovering Eternal Spirit of Allah,
and this is the inward grace through faith which
the *sibghat Allah* signifies.

Some Muslims, although they believe
that Isa is the Messiah,
are at first so filled with fear and confusion
that they do not want to rush into the *sibghat Allah* water.
When a Muslim receives Isa as Messiah
he can keep it quiet for awhile
until he grows in the Lord
and discerns who is trustworthy to be a witness
at his *sibghat Allah.*
No Muslim has to take the *sibghat Allah* immediately.
God in his mercy will permit one like Nicodemus

---

[1] Some believers interpret Colossians 2:11-12 to mean that a water initiation rite is the New Covenant counterpart to Old Covenant circumcision. To those believers the wudu would be an acceptable contextualized form However, these are not at all the issues this book intends to settle, and there is no time or space to pause for comment.

or Joseph of Arimathea
to come "secretly for fear" of his own people.¹

But it is hazardous and folly
to pamper oneself indefinitely in this disobedient state.
For Isa is Lord and he commands the water obedience.
The fear of man brings a snare,²
and whoever loves his family or anything in this world
more than the Messiah
is not worthy of the Messiah.³
"If we suffer, we shall also reign with him:
if we deny him, he also will deny us."⁴

Those who know of the *tariqa* (way) of *Khalq Jadeed* Muslims
know that the end of the way through
is to submit in total obedience to Allah.
Allah wants us to acknowledge our inability to have
a relationship with God by our own power.
In faith it is the power of our old sinful flesh
that must be drowned "in a sea of forgetfulness"
by the grace of the Spirit of Allah,
through our *sibghat Allah* faith obedience.

For Isa the *sibghat Allah* was a *wudu* (ablution) of consecration
that he took in preparation for his prayers
in the mountain of Temptation.
Just as Adam was tempted by Satan
and became the head of a lost *ummah* (community)
corrupted by a sin-nature leading to death,
so the New Adam, Isa,
who is after the "similitude...of Adam"⁵
was also tempted by Satan,
and became the head of a saved *ummah* (community),

---

¹John 19:38
²Proverbs 29:25
³Matthew 10:37
⁴II Timothy 2:12
⁵House of Imran 3:59

freed from the power of sin and sanctified for eternal life.
Isa did not believe that the water itself
had any power to ward off demons,
nor did he believe that any charm containing the bloodless word
of men could make Satan flee.
Isa did not use the water of his *wudu* (ablution)
to resist the devil.
He was filled with the eternal Spirit of Allah
and he took his stand on the Word of Allah,
and having stood all, he was able to stand.

Isa al-Masih, when He obeyed God
by submitting to the *sibghat Allah,*
went under the water as a prophetic act
to show the world what he would do:
he was going to die and be buried,
and then he was going to rise again.

We who are messianic Muslims
do not believe in baptismal regeneration.
Only God can regenerate us with the new birth miracle.
No amount of water can do it.
Only God can send the Eternal Holy Spirit
to cleanse a wicked heart with the waters of eternal life.
"Who can say, I have made my heart clean,
I am pure from my sin?" (Proverbs 20:9)

Nor do we believe that we can cleanse ourselves
by legalistic washings and endless rules of religion.
If we put ourselves under laws
we did not receive from Isa al-Masih,
and if we refuse to submit to Isa as Allah's Holy Word,
we shall die in our sins,[1]
in a state of spiritual uncleanness (*najasa*).

By faith (*iman*) we go under the water
believing that we are dead to the old inner man
and will become a new creation with a new inner man
when we rise to live,

---

[1] John 8:24

with sin no longer
in control of our lives.[1]

This is God's way of circumcising the inner person,
and who can baptize better than Allah?[2]

We who are new creation Muslims do not get our faith
from nominal religionists and the traditions of men.
For unregenerate men who lack the new creation
are not kinsmen (*junub*) of Isa,
and love to use religion to hide from obedience to the Word.
Isa said,
"Full well you reject the commandment of Allah
that you may keep your own tradition.
Whoever is ashamed of Isa and his blood and the Spirit of Allah
that he poured out on his *ummah* (community)
—whoever is ashamed of this Word Isa
and this Spirit, the Eternal Spirit
and this God, the true God, Allah,
—whoever is ashamed of this one true God,
in whose likeness we were created
both with Word and with Spirit,
—whoever is ashamed of this holy God,
of such a one this holy God will be ashamed
when we stand before Him to be judged by his Everlasting Word."

It is important to remember
that according to the Bible, an ordinance
is a symbolic rite instituted by Isa al-Masih.
There are two: immersion in the proper name of God
and a communion meal in remembrance of Isa.
One ordinance signifies the initiation of the covenant,
and the other renews it.
Of the two ordinances,
the first communion meal was celebrated in secrecy.
Why? Because of enemies and spies,
one of whom (Judas) managed to intrude into the rite,

---

[1] Romans 6:1-12
[2] Cow.2:138

though he was a false brother and a devil,
but it was necessary that prophecy be fulfilled.

Therefore, whoever says that an ordinance can not be
secret and private in times of danger
does not know much about the New Testament.

At the time of danger after the persecution
following the martyrdom of Stephen,
who witnessed the *sibghat Allah* of the Ethiopian eunuch
but Philip who administered the ordinance as its only witness?

Martyrdom is not to be encouraged.
Isa instructed his disciples to be wise as serpents
but as harmless as doves
and not to cast pearls before dangerous people
who would turn and try to tear them
with such precious personal information.[1]

My ethical problem is whether I will obey the Lord
and take *sibghat Allah.*
The ritual itself need not even be discussed with someone
who translates it as an "act of a traitor."
The holy things of the Lord are not for outsiders.
Such a person needs to understand and yield to salvation
before he is ready to hear about *sibghat Allah,*
which comes after and not before salvation.

Jesus cast no pearls before Pilate, Herod, or Caiaphas,
and these swine were amazed at his silence.
But he knew what was in a man,
whether his heart was open or whether he was dangerous.
and he needed no one to tell him what was in a person.
So it is with our *sibghat Allah.*
We who are the leaders in the messianic Muslim movement
do not invite Judas-type witnesses to our *sibghat Allah*
or to our messianic *Id ul-Adha* services
who will return with the police to destroy the flock.

---

[1] See also I Corinthians 10:29, which also throws light on the ethics of this question, and my obligation to discuss it with the ignorant.

The New Creation Pilgrimage

We keep the wrong people away
and we have a security screening system
such as we see Jesus using in John 12:20ff.

Only sympathetic and trustworthy believers
who have been carefully studied and examined
by those gifted with the ability to discern spirits
can take part in the *Id ul-Adha* sevice.

You should discuss this privately
with the leader of your fellowship
and trust the Lord that he will protect you.
Pray and ask the Lord for discernment and he will show you
who is trustworthy.
In the beginning,
new believers are sometimes
either fearful of everyone (paranoid)
or overly trusting of everyone (naive).
The Lord will show you how to avoid either
of these extremes
and to have his wisdom;
if you ask believing, He will answer.[1]
We do not have to tell everyone
in the messianic congregation
about your *sibghat Allah,*
just the ones you want to know.
The leader who administers it, if he is a godly man,
is the only witness you need have.

However, remember that the rite ceremonially
initiates you into the body of Messiah,
so there should be some connection with it
and a fellowship where the Word is rightly taught,
where the ordinances are rightly administered,
and where discipline is rightly conducted.

A SIBGHAT ALLAH SERVICE DESCRIBED

Perhaps you know little about

---

[1] James 1:5-6

Kalimat Allah Islam
and know very few new creation (*khalq jadeed*) Muslims.
You may not even have ever witnessed
a *sibghat Allah* ceremony.

Imagine if you will
a few Muslims with their imam.
He is the one who leads them in their prayers
and is their spiritual guide (*murshid*)
to keep them
on the straight path (*sirat mustaqim*).
The imam is the elder (*sheikh*)
and often the overseer (*muraqib*) or senior elder
of their place of assembly (*mujtama'*).

Now imagine these Muslims,
that is, the imam and the candidate (*mutarabbis*)
or aspirant for *sibghat Allah*.
Whether he or she is the only candidate at the ceremony
or there are others to take the ceremony with him or her,
it is the same ceremony in any case.[1]
They may or may not have witnesses.
The Imam himself is sufficient witness.
Certainly no one should be there who may turn out to be
a Judas and inform the religious authorities.
The ceremony may at times of danger be as private
as the Lord's Supper was at a similar time,
for on that night Isa al-Masih
was hidden from the eyes of all wicked men
with his small flock of a dozen disciples.
No one who could hurt them was allowed to know
where the ceremony took place or who the participants were.
It took an inside informer, Judas,
to make the whereabouts of the ceremony
a matter of information for the enemies of Isa.

---

[1] The mode described here is presented because it is symbolically appropriate for Muslims. However, there is no argument here that other forms are illegitimate, and no attempt here to throw the integrity of other believers in question because they have different understandings of the Biblically permissible forms believers may practice.

The New Creation Pilgrimage

The men who were with Isa
appreciated his efforts to protect them.
However, one of these disciples (*hawari*), John,
wrote later in Revelation 21:8
that cowards will find themselves in the lake of fire.
The main reason Judas left the secret ceremony
and would not involve himself in it any further,
was because he was a coward
who feared that Jesus (and he) would be killed.
Therefore, he tried to save his life
by betraying Isa to the authorities.
"But whoever would save his life will lose it,
and whoever will lose his life
(totally entrust it to the guardian-care of Isa)
will save it and keep it for eternity." (Mark 8:35)

Therefore, the Muslim candidate (*mutarabbis*)
or candidates have thoroughly counted the cost
when they meet with their imam
in a secluded place for the *sibghat Allah* ceremony.

Romans 6:4 says we are buried with him in the *sibghat Allah*.

Now, everyone should know that when a Muslim is buried
his body is given a special burial washing.
This is called a *ghusl*.

In the *ghusl* every impurity is to be removed from the body
and water is supposed to moisten
every part of the body and hair.
The ritual washing of the corpse is called *ghusl*,
and this is a very definite part of the preparation
of the body for interment.
A dead man can no longer sin.
His body ceases sinning and can be washed once and for all.
This is the point made in Romans 6.
We declare our bodies dead
as far as this satanic age is concerned.
We identify with the body of Isa which was put to death
so that by God's grace (unmerited favor),
our bodies could enter into the same death
and cease serving *Shaitan* (Satan) in this wicked world.

Listen to the argument again in the passage:
"What shall we say then?
Shall we continue in sin (*gayy*),
that grace (*ni`ma*) may abound?
Allah forbid!
How can we that are dead to sin
live any longer in it?
Do you not know that so many of us
as were brought under submission
to *sibghat* into Isa al-Masih
were baptized into His death?
Therefore we are buried with him
by baptism into death:
that just as al-Masih
was raised up from the dead
by the glory of Allah,
even so we also should walk
in newness of life."

When Isa was buried in his own *sibghat Allah,*
he was identifying with sinful man.
He is the *Wahid* Allah,
the Unique One of Allah,
is sinless, comes from Allah,
and is His everlasting Word (*Kalimatahoo al-azaliyaty*)
who will judge the living and the dead.

However, when he walked out into the water
at the river Jordan
it was as though the Judge of all men
was putting on a prisoner's uniform,
and beginning the process of becoming
the vicarious substitute who would
take the place of this condemned-to-hell human race.
He is the *Wahid* Allah
because he alone lacks a human father.
He alone lacks the nature of our sin-prone fathers,
because he alone of all men is the very Word of Allah.
Other prophets heard the Word of Allah
but he alone *is* the Word of Allah,
and as the Word of Allah
he is the Word of Judgment.

Therefore, Allah in his great justice (*qist*)
sent the Word of his Judgment himself
to be our substitute
and to mercifully stand in for us (*badil*).
Therefore Allah provided in his great mercy (*rahma*)
that instead of we who are guilty
being arrested,
put on trial,
sentenced,
and executed
to die and to be separated from Allah
and to descend into hell,
—instead of this—
the merciful Word of our judgment took our place.
> He, who was innocent and pure and unworthy of judgment,
> took the whole weight of our condemnation on himself.
> He was arrested in our place,
> he was put on trial in our place,
> he was sentenced in our place,
> he was executed in our place,
> he died in our place,
> he was separated from Allah in our place,
> he descended into sheol in our place.

This is what Isa meant when he spoke to
John the Baptist (*Yahya*) that day.
John was calling the heirs of Ibrahim
to submit to *sibghat Allah* in preparation for the world Judge
who was coming on the scene, the Messiah.

Yahya the precursor (*farat*) of Isa
preached repentance to an evil and adulterous world.
Yahya accused everyone, even the ultra-religious,
of being unclean before Allah.
He preached a *ghusl* (total ritual ablution of the body) of repentance,
demanding that everyone surrender to Allah
through the *sibghat Allah* which he preached.
The self-righteous person,
too proud to admit he is *junub* in his heart
(guilty of major impurity)
would not obey Allah's word through *Yahya*.

The ultra-religious of his day,
the mullahs of the sect of the Pharisees,
would not submit to his ghusl.
They considered themselves secure
in their religious *gnosis* (knowledge)
and in the praise they got from men
for their religious good deeds,
and they were not seeking the praise
that comes from God alone.
Yahya warned the whole religious establishment of his day
that all such hypocritical religious snakes
would be thrown by the Messiah the Judge (*Masih al-Hakam*)
into the eternal fire.

When John saw Isa coming
to take the *sibghat Allah* from him,
he said that he (John) should rather be baptized by Isa,
John knew that even though he was a prophet he was still
very much a sinner by nature,[1]
as is every sin-prone child of his sin-prone parents.
But Isa was the Word of Allah himself
and there is no sin in the Word of Allah.
However, Isa answered John this way:
"Allow it to be so now:
for thus it becometh us
to fulfill all righteousness."
Isa meant that sinners could be accounted righteous,
and righteousness could be made complete
only if Allah's righteous Word
personally suffered a death for the wicked.
Only then could the wicked enter into that death,
and, repenting, die to wickedness,
and come alive to true holy life
through the spiritual new birth.
Only the righteous Word of our judgment
could become this substitute, this replacement (*'iwadan*).

---

[1] Who would assert that all prophets are sinless? See Psalm 51:5. Just as the penalty of sin—death—is hereditary from the first Man, so is the sense of solidarity in the guilt of the first Man. See Romans 5 and Genesis 3.

The New Creation Pilgrimage

He was the only one who is the Word of Allah
and therefore he was qualified to make compensation for us.
He paid with his death the price
for our sins (*'ada'u*).
He gave a just and merciful exchange:
his sinless life given in death
which he did not deserve
was exchanged for our death-deserving sin;
and the gift was given to us of eternal life
which we do not deserve.

All of this was so clear to him at the time
of his *sibghat Allah*.
And later he explained to his disciples (*hawari*),
in a cryptic prophetic allusion to his death in *al-Quds:*
"But I have a baptism (referring to a total immersion
into suffering that was coming to him shortly)
to be baptized with,
and how I am straitened (distressed)
till it be accomplished!" (Luke 12:50)

Imagine an imam and a *Khalq Jadeed* Muslim
approaching the water in a secluded place
such as where the Lord's Supper was celebrated.

Imagine the joy of the occasion
but also the seriousness,
because we cannot
enter into the new creation life of the Word of Allah
unless we enter into his death.

Imagine that the imam and the new creation Muslims
are wearing white
and that the white they are wearing represents
the burial shroud that was on the body
of the totally submitted One,
the Word of Allah.
However, it represents also the *ihram*,
the pilgrim garb for pilgrimage into the new creation.
Isa himself is the object (*mahajja*) of our pilgrimage,
as he said, "I am the right way, the Straight path,
the mahajja as-sawab."

He lives in the House of Allah
not made by human hands but by Allah's Spirit
through whom He makes a new creation
out of all true believers (*mu'minin*).
We must discern his body, the house of Allah
wherein dwells his mystical presence,
and we must discern him,
when we relate to fellow believers.

We are starting on a pilgrimage
and our *sibghat Allah* represents its beginning.
The Word of Allah requires this of us
as our first act of obedience.
So how can we begin the pilgrimage,
if we have not obeyed even the first commandment?

You have heard the saying:
"My Lord hath commanded Justice (*qist*)
and that ye set your whole selves to Him."[1]
You have also heard the saying:
God has bestowed on the children of Adam
"a raiment of righteousness"
to cover their shame.[2]
Since God's justice (*qist*) demands
that the guilty not go unpunished[3]
and since his mercy
has given us a means of covering our shame,
we who are *Khalq Jadeed* (New Creation) Muslims
put on Isa himself as our raiment of righteousness
when we rise out of the water
to begin our pilgrimage,
a journey on which we are being transformed
into his likeness
with ever-increasing glory
which comes from the Lord,

---

[1] Heights. 7:29
[2] Heights. 7:26
[3] Nahum 1:3 NIV

The New Creation Pilgrimage

who is the Spirit.[1]

It says in the Qur'an
that "the pagans are unclean"[2]
but it takes more than religion or water ablutions
to make one truly Muslim.
For many who say they are Muslim
are pagans at heart,
and look clean on the outside of the cup
but inside are filled with every kind of hypocrisy.
Only the inner tahara of the new birth
can remove the inner pagan uncleanness
and make one a spiritual submitter (*Muslim*) within.

Isa says that wherever two or more
are gathered in his name,
there He is in the midst of them
for koinonia or mystic converse.
The word for this most Muslims hear all the time
but do not understand it.
Near Mount Sinai, Moses drew near to God
for mystic converse (*najiy*).[3]
Unfortunately, this is a word that is not widely understood.
It carries the idea
of communication or connection (*ittisaal*).
When we have mystic converse or koinonia,
we have *ittisaal*.
We are in connection for communication with Allah.
At the upper room during the Last Supper
Judas ate bread with the rest,
but it was not changed in his wicked mouth.
Nor is there any power in the water of *sibghat Allah*
or in the bread of the New Creation *Id ul-Adha*.
The power is in the *ittisaal*, in the *najiy*,
in the koinonia, in the mystic converse,
in the connection, in the communication with Allah.

---

[1] II Corinthians 3:18 NIV
[2] Repentance. 9:28
[3] Maryam. 19:52

There is another meaning in this word.
It has to do with fellowship or comradeship (*zamala*).
Believers experience the *zamala* in the comradeship
of being partakers and partners in the grace
of the Good News.
It is a comradeship in the Spirit.
Now, men in an army
know what esprit de corps (*'asabiya*) is,
and in any organization or group,
religious or otherwise,
such a feeling of team spirit is not unheard of.
However, *zamala* (comradeship) in the Eternal Spirit
is a comradeship with the Word of Allah himself.
It means experiencing his sufferings and his joys
and his vision and his victories with him.
Judas experienced the bread of the Lord's feast (*id*)
and the water of the *sibghat Allah*
but he did not experience the *zamala*.
Judas experienced the water of *sibghat Allah*
as did all the other disciples (*hawari*)
but he did not experience *zamala*.

Here we are talking about a spiritual knowledge.
Koinonia is not *fiqh*, the exercise of the intelligence
or the legal mind.
It is not *`arif*, that so-called knowledge
of the mystical knower
who thinks he apprehends God
by immediate experience and vision
but without the new birth of regeneration through Isa.

Koinonia is the knowledge (*'ilm*) of regeneration (*nahda*)
known only by the new creation children of God
who cry "Abba, Father!" in the power of the Eternal Spirit
and know God with a new intimacy through His Word Isa
not possible without the new birth.

THE TRUE STORY OF AHMAD

The secret ceremony that Judas was too afraid
to get really involved in was called the Lord's Supper,
but we call it the *'Id ul-'Adha 'Isawiya*,

because of its deep relationship to pilgrimage
and covenant and submission to Allah through Ibrahim
and the sacrifice of his heir.

But what a fool Judas was!
He would have died anyway,
and very shortly at that in this dangerous world.
If only he had made the brief time left to him
in his fleeting life
a brave witness for Isa
by fully taking part in this secret ceremony,
instead of cowardly avoiding it.
Now he must spend endless ages in the anguish of hell.
So what did he save?
Did he save his life through cowardice?
Allah forbid that any of our Muslim brothers
should refuse to receive Isa as Allah's Word
because they are too cowardly to obey his commandment
to submit to the *sibghat Allah*.
Endless ages from now,
when they groan in endless anguish,
they will regret forever
this cowardly error.[1]

Here is the testimony of Ahmad,
whom God gave the grace not to be cowardly.
This is a true testimony
in his own words.

AHMAD TELLS HIS OWN STORY

I had been raised as a Muslim in a very Muslim house for the first eighteen years that I was at home. Later, as an adult, I

---

[1]This does not mean that anyone who has not taken the death *ghusl* of Isa is automatically going to hell. It does mean, however, that anyone who says that he believes in Isa and yet refuses to submit to his command—Matthew 28:19-20—regarding this ordinance is in danger of coming under the judgment of the Word of God: "The man who says, 'I know him', while he disobeys his commands, is a liar and a stranger to the truth"—I John 2:4. "Whoever runs ahead and does not continue in the teaching of the Messiah does not have God"—II John 9.

started hearing about Jesus. According to the Qur'an I had believed that Jesus was one of God's prophets.

As time went on, I started hearing more and more about him, how he died for the human race to set men free from sin, sickness and every bondage. Prior to hearing all this, I had always wondered about sickness and disease and why God would take so many people at a very young age or put sickness on them. If mankind is God's masterpiece, I always wondered what kind of Creator would create a masterpiece and then watch his masterpiece deteriorate without doing something about it.

I kept saying to myself, "God, I love you and I have been brought up to worship you, but I don't know anything about *Isa* (Jesus)." This went on for about three years.

In January, 1982, I had started my own business. Two months later, my wife and I made an agreement to sit down and read the Bible and find out firsthand who Isa is and what he has done for the human race. As we read the Bible, I was amazed to see that it is just as true as I had been told. We continued to read the Bible for several weeks and at the same time we were listening to teaching tapes about the Bible.

I read the Word of God in John 3:3, "Truly, truly, I say to you, unless one is born again he cannot see the Kingdom of God." Isa was simply saying that we are born of flesh and blood. However, unless we are born of the Spirit of Isa al-Masih and come to know God personally, we can not see the Kingdom of God.

My wife and I were stirred by Romans 10 where it says "if you confess with your mouth Isa as Lord and believe in your heart that God raised him from the dead, you shall be saved." Right at that point my wife and I knew that in our hearts a change was taking place. Until then I did not know of any way to change our sinful nature and to be acceptable to God without trying to earn a right standing by being religious. I knew that God was speaking to us, but I was confused.

Then it was as if God was speaking to my heart and saying, "You are not denying anything, you are believing in the name of

The New Creation Pilgrimage

my Word, Isa al-Masih, whom I have sent into the world so that the world may be set free from sin. I have done this because I love the people, mankind whom I have created."

It was then that my wife and I made up our minds to believe. And right at that time, I could feel the joy of the Lord grasping my whole body as I realized that Isa had gone down to the pit to pay for our sins there and to carry away our sicknesses and diseases. Then we started reading the Bible regularly, listening to teaching tapes and not only reading and hearing the Word of God, but also making the decision to do the Word of God the way God said it and to live in it so that we could receive from God in the manner he had intended for us to receive from him.

Then so many good things started happening to us. My wife got healed from kidney problems, from swelling and from foot problems after we prayed in the name of Isa and believed that God's healing was for us.

As we continued to read the Bible we actually came closer and closer to God. We learned how to overcome problems by finding the answer and the promise and claiming it in his Word. Consequently, both our bodies and business have been blessed by the Lord. Not only that, but God has purified us by the study of his Word, so that instead of arguments and selfishness there has been peace and love in our home.

The Bible says that God has made Isa al-Masih our redemption, sanctification, righteousness, and wisdom. When you know that he is all this for us, you not only have the peace of the assurance of your salvation, you also can overcome all things that come against you.

For example, my Muslim friend, Mehmet, had just had brain surgery not long ago to remove a cancerous tumor. He was dying. He was sad. He was fearful. He didn't want to die, and he didn't think that God really wanted to take him at the age of 32. When I first ran into him, he told me that he was dying and he was so sad. I looked at him and I told him "Jesus can heal you." His response was "Who is that?"

After a while we got together, and I started sharing with him from the Word of God. I told him that Jesus had died for him, that Isa was sent to this world for his sake to set him free, that God was calling all people to Him through his Word Isa, and that when we believe in his name, we can be helped through every trial that befalls us.

Mehmet could not make the commitment right away. He was raised in a Muslim home and it took a while for the word of God to sink in. But as we shared, Mehmet started feeling inside of him that the Scriptures I showed him were the Word of God. He believed that somehow the truth could set him free. He finally said that he wanted to receive Isa as his Saviour so that Isa the Word of Allah would reign supreme in his heart. He did.

Several weeks later, when doctors examined him, he was completely healed.[1]

Miraculously healed with no evidence of cancer being left behind! Now Mehmet had the joy; his face was shining with joy and with glory and with the happiness that comes from knowing the Lord. When I ran into him again, all he could talk about was how good God is, how good his Word Isa is, and how he had been set free by believing in the name of Jesus.

I recently submitted to God by obeying him regarding the *sibghat Allah* and was immersed as He commands. This simple act signifies that my old life without him was buried in the water and my new life (and he is the source of that life) has been raised again with him as he made me a new person, a new creation, a Khalq Jadeed Muslim. Since I have obeyed the Lord in this, I have felt closer to God and closer to His Word. The *sibghat Allah* (baptism of God) is a simple remembrance of the death and resurrection of Isa al-Masih. Every time I remember that day and that simple act, I remember that I am set free from all the

---

[1] See footnote 3 on page 125 in The New Creation Confession. God is sovereign and heals sovereignly, and His ways are higher than our ways. We should avoid faithless unbelief when we need a healing, but we should also avoid creating simplistic formulas for God, as Job and other sections of Scripture warn us.

The New Creation Pilgrimage

bondages and all the shortcomings of this world through the overcoming power I have in Isa al-Masih.

My prayer is that other Muslims like Mehmet and I will inquire of the Word of God and receive Isa as the Word of Allah so that they too will receive the priceless joy and the power that overcomes the world. Amen.

WHY DELAY?

"Fulfill the Covenant of Allah
when you have entered into it."[1]

"And now, what doth the Lord require of thee?
To fear the Lord thy God,
to walk in his ways
(according to his infallibly accurate Word)
to love him,
and to serve the Lord thy God
with all thy heart
and with all thy soul,
to keep the commandments of the Lord
and his statutes." [2]

"See I have set before thee this day life and good,
and death and evil."[3]

Choose Life!

"But if your heart turn away
so that you will not hear,
but shall be drawn away,
and worship other gods,
and serve them,
I denounce unto you this day
that you shall surely perish,

---

[1] Bee. 16:91
[2] Deuteronomy 10:12-13
[3] Deuteronomy 30:15

and that you shall not prolong your days
upon the land."[1]

"Thou shalt love the Lord thy God
with all thy heart,
and with all thy soul,
and with all thy mind.
This is the first and great commandment.
And the second is like unto it,
Thou shalt love thy neighbor as thyself.
On these two commandments
hang all the law and the prophets."[2]

And it says that those who submitted to Allah through obedience in the *sibghat Allah* "continued steadfastly in the apostles' teaching (which is the infallibly accurate word of the Old and New Testament Scriptures, which the faithful scribes among them took care not to allow. to be changed or corrupted and which cannot be added to) and in the fellowship (which is worship and mutual service and sharing and edifying society among the brethren) and in breaking of bread (which is the messianic *Id ul-Adha* remembrance of Isa the Word of Allah's last pilgrimage meal) and in the prayers (which is prayer meeting, with prayer and fasting which the believers were commanded not to neglect)."[3]

These are Isa's commandments,
and those who take the *sibghat Allah*
are covenanting with the Lord
to obey his commandment
as he provides the grace and the strength.
Isa said,
"If you love me,
keep my commandments.
He that hath my commandments,
and keepeth them,

---

[1] Deuteronomy 30:17, 18
[2] Matthew 22:37-40
[3] Acts 2:42

he it is that loveth me."[1]

Isa said,
"Ye are my friends,
if you do whatsoever
I command you."[2]

"When ye shall have done
all those things
which are commanded you, say,
We are unprofitable servants:
we have done that which was our duty to do.."[3]

Do you understand that
after your *sibghat Allah* experience,
the Lord will expect you
to be faithful (as He provides both strength and opportunity)
in prayers and teaching and fellowship
with the other believers?

The Spirit of God gives us love for the brethren,
so you should feel a genuine love
and desire to be with fellow believers.
Without this love and commitment on your part
there can be no real expression of your life
as a genuine believer.
But with this love and commitment on your part,
there is the wonderful reality
that you have an international world-wide family
who call on the same Lord,
and know the same Spirit
and the same God.

The *wudu* of Isa or the *sibghat Allah* is a burial *ghusl*
for those who are dead to sin and alive to God through
Isa al-Masih, the eternal Word.
In Matthew 28:19 Isa commands

---

[1] John 14:15,21
[2] John 15:14
[3] Luke 17:10

that the repentant true believers of the whole world
take this prescribed *wudu*.
Isa said, "If you *love* me, keep my commandments."
The question is: Do you really love Isa?
Yes?
Well, he said,
"If you love me, keep my commandments." (John 14:15)
Do you sincerely desire to be truly submitted to Allah
as a true messianic Muslim student of Isa al-Masih?
Do you love Isa? Then follow His commandments.
Get the *wudu*. Get washed in His name,
trusting His blood to wash away your sins once and forever.
Then you will truly be prepared for your prayers
to a God who is faithful
as you are obedient to his faithfulness.
Then you will feel a new intimate communion
with Allah when you come to pray,
for you will know your sins
are covered and forgiven.
If you obey Isa,
God will give you an assurance of forgiveness
and a greater sense of the presence
of his Eternal Spirit in your life.
You will feel a deeper fellowship
not only with God but with other believers in Isa.

You have heard the saying,
"Whoever holds firmly to God
will be shown the way that is straight." [1]
If you really love Allah,
you will follow that straight way now,
no matter what it costs you.

SIBGHAT ALLAH ACCEPTANCE PRAYER

"Praise be to God, the Lord of the worlds:
Most Gracious, most merciful:
Master of the Day of Judgment.
You do we worship and your aid we seek.

---

[1] House of Imran. 3:101

The New Creation Pilgrimage

Show us the straight path,
the path of those
on whom you have bestowed your grace.
Those whose portion is not wrath,
and who do not go astray.

Isa, the sovereign and eternal Word
risen from the grave to the right hand of power in heaven,
I obey you absolutely that I may continue in Allah's good pleasure.

Help me to judge myself
so that I will not be judged
when I stand before your throne.
Help me to study and understand and obey your holy commands
in fellowship with your faithful followers.

I accept the *wudu* of Isa, his burial *ghusl*, the *sibghat Allah*,
as a small test of my faith and obedience to my Masih,
Isa the Word of Allah.
I will submit to God's will.
I agree to take the *sibghat Allah*
once as a *wudu* to prepare for a life-time
of calling out to Allah (*du'a*) in free prayer.
And I will take the *sibghat Allah*
in the name of God
and His Eternal Word Isa
and His Eternal Spirit.
I trust that I will be blessed
by being more submitted to Allah with my whole being.
Thank you forever, Heavenly Father, in the name of Isa al-Masih,
that you have cleansed me and made me pure in Your Eternal Spirit
by the blood of Isa as my acceptable sacrifice from Allah.
Amen."

A NEW CREATION MUSLIM *SIBGHAT ALLAH* SERVICE

"Our Lord! forgive us
our sins and anything
we may have done

that transgressed our duty:
establish our feet firmly,
and help us against those
who resist faith."[1]

"Not by works of righteousness
which we have done,
but according to his mercy
he saved us,
by the washing of regeneration (the new birth)
and the renewing of the Eternal Spirit of Holiness;
which he shed on us abundantly
through Isa al-Masih our Saviour."[2]

Water is the outward and visible sign,
and the regeneration of the new birth
is the inward and spiritual grace
of the *sibghat Allah*,
which signifies the remission of sins.[3]
We who are sons of Ibrahim by faith
gather together at this place of water
to submit ourselves to Allah according to his Word,
Isa al-Masih.

The white we wear symbolizes our pilgrim status
as we begin a life of obedience
unto the *tariqa* (way) of holiness,
which is a life we share together in Him.

We confess that mere water
cannot give us the status of *tahara* (undefilement),
since only the Eternal Spirit can circumcise away
our spiritual uncleanness and can cut away
the pull of our lower nature
and the lusts that pull us down.
Yet Allah has promised to provide this spiritual *tahara*
if we will obey his Word Isa al-Masih

---

[1] House of Imran. 3:147
[2] Titus 3:5,6
[3] Acts 22:16

The New Creation Pilgrimage

with an undivided heart.
The Word of Allah, Isa al-Masih,
commands us to be immersed and buried with him.
This is our acceptable preparation for *'ibadat* (worship).

To the candidate (*mutarabbis*):
    Do you confess that you are a sinner,
    and that Isa al-Masih is the only way
    your sins can be forgiven
    and that you can know
    you have forgiveness and eternal life in God?

Candidate: I do.

(This is the time when a personal testimony would be appropriate. "And I say unto you, whosoever shall confess me before men, him shall the Son of Man also confess before the angels of God: But he that denieth me before men shall be denied before the angels of God."—Luke 12:8,9; Mt.10:32. "If thou shalt confess the Lord *Isa* (Jesus) and shalt believe in thine heart that God has raised him from the dead, thou shalt be saved. For with the heart man believeth unto righteousness: and with the mouth confession is made unto salvation."—Romans 10:9,10. "For we ourselves also were sometimes foolish, disobedient, deceived, serving all kinds of passions and pleasures, living in malice and envy, hateful, and hating one another. But after that the kindness and love of God our Saviour toward man appeared. Not by works of righteousness which we have done, but according to his mercy he saved us, by the washing of regeneration, and renewing of the Holy Spirit, which he shed on us abundantly through Isa al-Masih our Savior; that being justified by his grace, we should be made heirs according to the hope of eternal life." —Titus 3:3-7.)

To the candidate:

    Repeat after me,
    Lord, I confess all my sins before you right now.
    And I thank you that Isa al-Masih paid for them all
    by his precious blood so that I can become clean
    and join the family of the redeemed as a child of God
    who is my loving heavenly Father.

I repent and renounce all my sins
and I promise before this witness that by His strength
I will never turn back to my sins
or intentionally grieve the Eternal Holy Spirit.
I believe that there is one God
Who infallibly revealed himself
with the personal distinctions of God
and His Word and His Spirit
with the one name of Father
and Filial Word and Eternal Spirit.
I do *not* believe that God took a wife
in order that Isa could become his son through Mary.
I believe that his Eternal Word, incarnated as Isa,
was always with God and was always God
and therefore that the Eternal Word
always knew God as Eternal Father.

Today I am entering into a covenant
which this water rite initiates through faith,
and I am promising God in this solemn ceremony
that I will be a faithful part of his family forever,
not forsaking the assembling of those
who are *khalq jadeed* (new creation) submitters to Allah.

When I pass through this water rite,
I will be formally welcomed as a member
of the *khalq jadeed ummah* (community)
of true believers in the *Wahid* Allah,
the Unique One of Allah, Isa al-Masih.

To the candidate:
   Do you solemnly promise that you will remember
   and renew this covenant initiated in water
   by assembling for the celebration of the messianic *Id ul-Adha*
   with your brothers and sisters in the faith,
   and that you will zealously study the faith
   once for all inerrantly recorded in the Scriptures
   and that you will pray that God will open a door
   for you to share your faith and serve Him in it?
(In some cases the male candidates may want
to wear the prayer hat called the *targheer*

or the *koofi* or *koofayah*.
The prayer robe is called the *galibeers*.
This would symbolize that he is not changing
religious labels and would point to
the new creation. The point of the rite is
not assimilation away from the familiar
but newness of life within the familiar.)[1]

---

[1] I Corinthians 11:4 doesn't refer to a hat, which Paul knew very well was worn by the High Priest—see Exodus 28:4—but to the Corinthian tendency to take him literally when he said there is no difference between male and female. To preach this, the men were apparently wearing their wives' veils and scandalizing local custom.

New Creation Book for Muslims 6

Starting a house Masjid and a messianic Madrasa

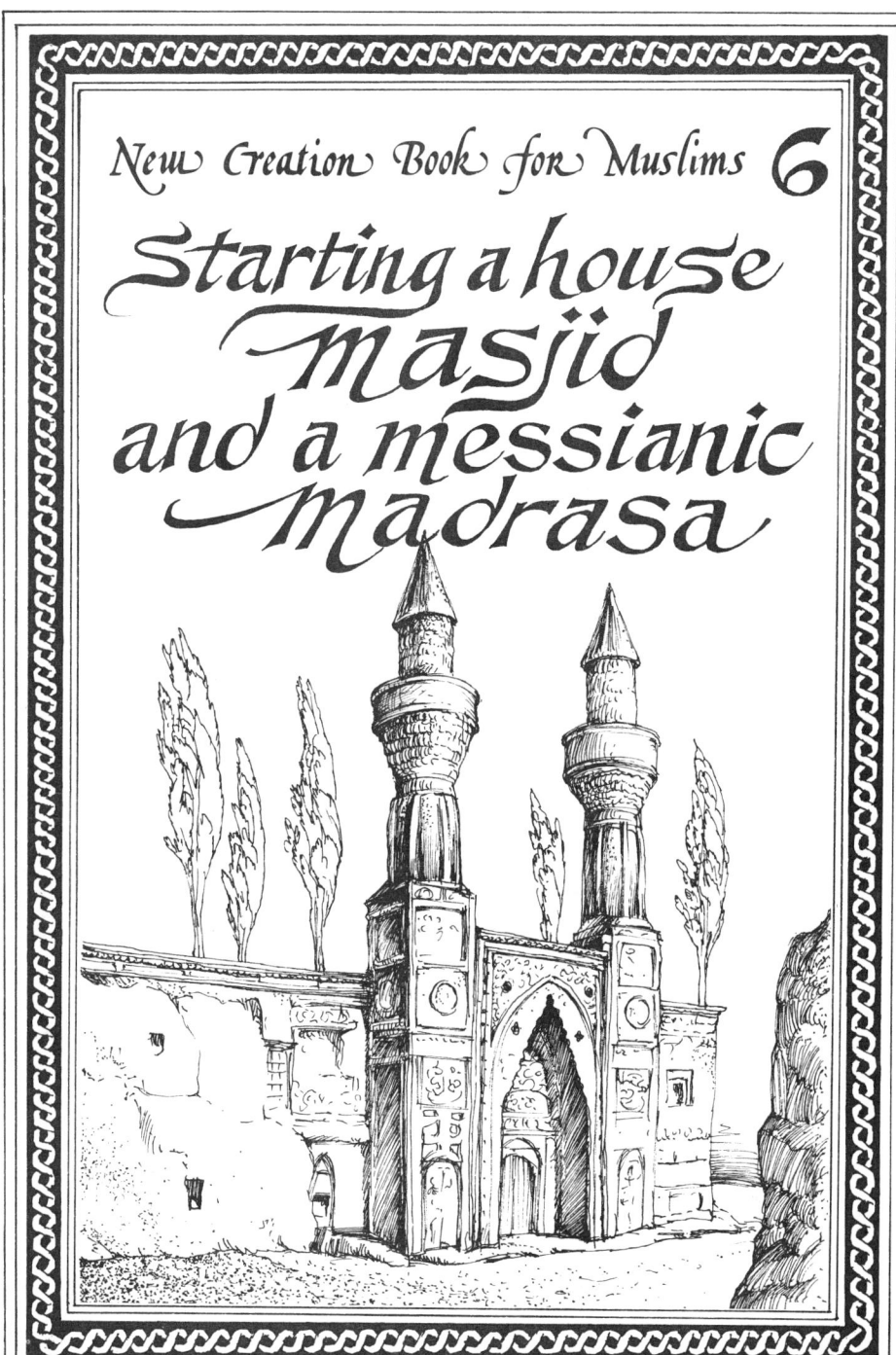

6

How to Start a House Masjid for New Creation Muslims

Imagine, if you will, an ordinary house in a secluded place at the edge of town. It is Thursday and the week-end is fast approaching. The urgent question is, how can this house be transformed into a house *masjid* for the weekend new creation Muslim fellowship meeting?

Imagine walking through the front door. On your right is a bathroom, a perfect place for the believers to wash after they take off their shoes and put on their head coverings. Some shelves or racks in this area would be helpful, for the believers to put coats and shoes and other belongings aside in an orderly way.

As you walk into the front room, you notice two things: there is a distinct lack of western furniture and there are no images of any kind on the walls. The floor is totally covered with Oriental carpets, and there are floor cushions and pillows bordering the walls, but no tables and chairs. On the walls, instead of pictures of any kind, there are various poster designs utilizing Arabic calligraphy and quoting key messianic passages from the Qur'an such as are emphasized in this book (see footnote #1 on page 10 in the *Soiltesting* book).

This is the front room. It can serve as a social hall as believers are gathering before the main meetings. It can become a dining room by setting up low, portable tables in a horseshoe configuration, with the guests sitting on the floor, being served Muslim-style ethnic foods and tea in small Middle Eastern tea cups and saucers, etc. Or the low portable dining tables can be taken out, and the room's floorspace is now cleared again for the "afterglow" time of spiritual chants, antiphonal hymns, solos, and Sufi-style liturgical dance to the accompaniment of Middle Eastern drum, cymbals, etc.

A second large room in the house could be similarly furnished and decorated for use both as a place of teaching/preaching and prayer. The *imam* or *sheikh* could preach or teach from a seated position (possibly on a floor cushion in a Mecca-directioned corner of the room) with the believers sitting on the floor and the Arabic Scriptures opened toward them on a low book stand. The women could sit together on one side of the room and the men could sit on the other side, so that the women are not distracting their line of vision. The women could wear head scarfs and modest, non-alluring clothing, and the men could wear the white prayer hat (*koofi*). The call to prayer could be made at the hall doorway leading out of the prayer room into the fellowship room.

A possible order of service for a week-end evening meeting could go something like this. The believers arrive, removing coats and shoes, donning prayer hats. After a time of informal social fellowship, the believers assemble in a prayer circle and chant their confession. The confession is given in English and Arabic in the section entitled, *The Prayer Life of a New Creation Muslim.* The confession states:

"I bear witness that Isa is the Word of God,
who sendeth forth the (Eternal) Spirit,
proceeding from the command (*Amr*) of my Lord,
Isa the Messiah, His Word,
the ransom of all Ibrahim's heirs and our momentous sacrifice,
raised to Allah, as a warning of the Day of Meeting,
that He might put away our evil-prone flesh,
and bring a new creation, even righteousness by faith alone."

How to Start a Concealed House Masjid 173

All these phrases are found in the Qur'an and can be set to an Islamic style melody by anyone who is musically inclined and would take the trouble to study a recording such as "Calling Out to Allah; Prayers and Chants in the Sufi Tradition, the Halveti-Jerrahi Dervishes." (This is purchaseable by writing Inner Traditions International, Ltd. 377 Park Ave. South, New York City, New York 10016).

Then the believers could break out of the prayer circle and could file into the prayer room for a time of Scripture teaching and prayer. A sample service is provided in the section entitled, *The Prayer Life of a New Creation Muslim*. For help with the Arabic in this section, it is recommended that one order both the book and the tapes that accompany the book entitled, *The Prescribed Prayer Made Simple*, by Tajuddin B. Shu'aib. (This can be ordered from Da'awah Enterprises International, Inc. P.O. Box 43554, Los Angeles, CA. 90043)

After the teaching and prayer service are concluded, the believers can go into the fellowship hall and have a common meal together. Those who break bread together during the *'Id ul-'Adha Isawiya* portion of the meal can witness to the unbelievers present. (A large bathtub somewhere in the house can be used for the *sibghat Allah* ceremony whenever it is deemed advisable to cautiously proceed with it, possibly in private.) It is assumed, of course, that no unbeliever would be brought to this type of meeting unless he or she had been thoroughly screened and was considered a "safe" guest.

After the fellowship meal is concluded and tea has been served, the tables can be put away. For those who are of a Sufi dervish background, this could be an "afterglow" time of chanting, liturgical dance, and making spiritual melodies to the Lord. This worship session is the climax of the evening, and should be done decently and in order. The liturgical dance movements should be carried out in an orderly and aesthetically pleasing mode, devoid of sensuality or fleshly emotional display. The women should form one circle and the men another. The movements can be performed while seated in a circle on the floor with the leader to be imitated raising his hands, etc., in the middle of the circle. Or the believers can stand and, holding hands or swaying together or putting their arms around each others' shoulders or walking in a circular direction or crossing one leg in front of the other, they can sing either together or as an antiphonal response to a soloist. Excessive frenzy or hyperventilating or giddiness stimulated by constant group head turning or heavy breathing should be avoided. A Scriptural study of the use of dance and music in worship will show that the exhilirating joy of the presence of the Spirit of the Lord can be experienced by regenerated believers in orderly worship without physical manipulations or unspiritual excesses. Worshippers should guard against excess both in the prohibition and expresssion of this form of worship.

It is the prayer of Salim Munayer and Phil Goble (as well as a number of other cross-cultural ministers to Muslims who helped in the development of this book) that those who read these pages will be encouraged to form house *masjid* fellowships, perhaps initailly on a once-a-month-basis, but then, later on, on a weekly or more frequent basis. It is also our prayer that each house *masjid* will eventually have its own Islamic Academy (*Madrassa*) for New Creation Muslims so that leaders can be trained and sent out to start new house *masjids* in other areas throughout the world. Then we believe a Muslim people movement to Isa will begin, and New Creation Muslim communities will spring up all over the world with their own international congresses, youth conferences, schools, and special purpose organizations. Every time a regional conference raises up people burdened and equipped to plant new worshipping communities, a greater and greater international network will grow as the world-wide people movement catches fire.

The contextualized approach presented in this book, though by no means the only acceptable Scriptural model, holds great promise for encouraging an end-time world-wide people movement among the nearly one billion Muslims of the world into the New Creation *Ummah* of Ibrahim in these last days.

Glossary

Al-Faatihah	first sura of the Qur'an
al-Quds	Jerusalem
amr	command
du'a	supplications
ghusl	total ablution
'Id 'ul-Adha	the feast of Sacrifice
imam	spiritual leader
iman	faith
Injil	New Testament
Isa al-Masih	Jesus
jami'	congregation, gathering
jihad	struggle
jum'ah	Friday service
kaffarah	expiation, atonement
khutbah	sermon
masjid	place of prayer
Muaadhdhin	caller to prayer
sibghat Allah	baptism
Shaitan	Satan
tawhid	unity
sura	chapter (in the Qur'an)
ummah	the entire community of believers
wudu	ceremonial washing